DEPRESSION

EMPOWERING YOU

The Rowman & Littlefield Empowering You series is aimed to help you, as a young adult, deal with important topics that you, your friends, or family might be facing. Whether you are looking for answers about certain illnesses, social issues, or personal problems, the books in this series provide you with the most up-to-date information. Throughout each book you will also find stories from other teenagers to provide personal perspectives on the subject.

*For Alicia—thank you
for always believing in me
and my writing*

DEPRESSION

Insights and Tips for Teenagers

CHRISTIE COGNEVICH

ROWMAN & LITTLEFIELD
Lanham • Boulder • New York • London

Published by Rowman & Littlefield
An imprint of The Rowman & Littlefield Publishing Group, Inc.
4501 Forbes Boulevard, Suite 200, Lanham, Maryland 20706
www.rowman.com

6 Tinworth Street, London, SE11 5AL, United Kingdom

British Library Cataloguing in Publication Information Available

Library of Congress Cataloging-in-Publication Data

Names: Cognevich, Christie, 1984– author.
Title: Depression : insights and tips for teenagers / Christie Cognevich.
Description: Lanham : Rowman & Littlefield, [2020] | Series: Empowering you |
  Includes bibliographical references and index. | Audience: Ages 13–18 |
  Summary: "This book offers relatable situations and strategies to
  guide teens struggling with mental health—including identifying signs of
  struggle, recognizing stress factors, and offering strategies to escape
  harmful mental habits which can leave individuals feeling vulnerable,
  helpless, or in despair"— Provided by publisher.
Identifiers: LCCN 2020011184 (print) | LCCN 2020011185 (ebook) | ISBN
  9781538137604 (paperback) | ISBN 9781538137611 (epub)
Subjects: LCSH: Depression in adolescence—Juvenile literature.
Classification: LCC RJ506.D4 C63 2020 (print) | LCC RJ506.D4 (ebook) |
  DDC 616.85/2700835—dc23
LC record available at https://lccn.loc.gov/2020011184
LC ebook record available at https://lccn.loc.gov/2020011185

™
⊗ The paper used in this publication meets the minimum requirements of
American National Standard for Information Sciences—Permanence of Paper for
Printed Library Materials, ANSI/NISO Z39.48-1992.

CONTENTS

YOU ARE NOT ALONE

*D*epression: Insights and Tips for Teenagers is guided by anecdotes—brief stories told by people who have experienced the real-life issues they're discussing. All anecdotes in this book are from teenagers or someone describing their own experiences with depression as a teenager. That includes me.

I experienced depression all through my teenage years and beyond, sometimes having long stretches of healthiness and sometimes having long times of darkness varying in intensity depending on the day. I have gone through the ups and downs of not realizing what was going on with me, or realizing I was having a depressive episode but feeling helpless to do anything about it.

I've resisted therapy when I knew deep down that I would benefit from it, and I've gone through the complicated process of looking for therapists when I wasn't feeling well or motivated. I've had some very not-good fits in the therapy department, but I've also found great people I trust and with whom I feel safe talking. I've had (and sometimes still have) some unhealthy coping habits. I know what it's like when a bad choice feels like a warm hug at the moment and like shame afterward. Let's be honest: for me, that bad choice looks like too many tacos and a lot of regrets. I've also picked up a lot of useful coping skills along the way from a lot of wise people both in and out of the mental health profession.

There are many incredibly useful resources, workbooks, and guides out there written by experts in the field. Pick them up and take a look at them. If there's anything I've found in my years of working and struggling through my problems, it's that the more resources you see, the better. Wisdom and insight can come from the least expected places. I have learned so much from therapists, counselors, social workers, psychiatrists, and psychologists. I've also been inspired, and I've grown by talking with students in training in the mental health field. I've bonded and benefited from being with others who have depression, anxiety, and other mental health issues. Not everyone has been an expert in terms of having degrees and certifications, but they all had so many valuable things to share.

In the spirit of seeking insight everywhere, what distinguishes this book from others is that while doctors, counselors, and therapists write most of the other guides on depression out there, my experience with depression is personal, and my work with teenagers isn't with patients. I'm a teacher. I spend more than eight hours a day working side by side with amazing adolescents grappling with and overcoming all kinds of mental and physical struggles. One of the things I love most is how much I learn from and am inspired by my students.

As a teacher, one of the greatest gifts I can share with my students is not just literature (it's good for the soul!), but my experiences. Not because my experiences look just like theirs. Not because my experiences are the perfect models to follow, but because we're all humans trying to weave the rich tapestry of life that sometimes gets a little knotted and tangled.

I was born with moderate hearing loss. It runs in the family; my mother and uncles are deaf. Sometimes I was motivated to sit in the front row of class and pay extra attention to follow what was happening, and sometimes I just zoned out and doodled because I couldn't hear, and it was too exhausting to keep following. Sometimes my teachers forgot about my hearing, and I got in trouble for not paying attention when I asked something that had already been answered. Sometimes that made me feel unbearably stupid, so I just stopped raising my hand and asking questions. I hated my hearing aids. They made me feel self-conscious, so I went years without wearing them regularly (not good), and then I was so sensitive to sound when I did wear them that I got overstimulated and had to take them out all the time.

I had depression off and on for years. Left unacknowledged, it didn't improve. My habits for (not) dealing with it didn't improve either.

Now I have a PhD in English literature and a career I love, but when I first started college at eighteen, I dropped out after my first semester. I started again after transferring schools, changed my major, and dropped out again. There was also an awful hair decision between those two events, but we don't need to talk about that.

I felt like a failure.

Everyone else was out there living their best life, and I wasn't. All the things that kept me depressed at the time have added up to make me who I am now, writing this book. It didn't help to be told that whatever I was going through was going to be okay, or that whatever was happening was happening for a reason, or that it was all going to turn out for the best. I'm glad I get to share some of those experiences with you.

I've carried a lot of emotional pain, and I've tried to ignore it or keep it secret. I've made mistakes, and I've also made great choices to reach out for help from family, friends, and professionals. I have benefited from therapy, and I have benefited from medication. Now, I get to talk about it in the hopes of helping someone else. That's amazing. So let's talk!

My goal is that this should not feel like an advice book. Adults are all too willing to dispense advice (and some of it might even be excellent), but too often, advice comes flavored with a little layer of condescension or judgment. If you're reading this book, it's unlikely that brand of advice is what you want or need.

Truthfully, though I'm not a teenager anymore, I still chafe under advice. *If you just let it go and move on, you'll feel better. It's going to be okay. If you believe that, you'll feel better*—not my cup of tea.

Instead, I like to understand things better. When I understand, I can make better choices for myself. Maybe my weird choices that I get mad at myself about turn out to have made sense in the context of how our brains work. Understanding can be so calming.

I hope this book will serve that purpose for you.

PART I

WHAT IS DEPRESSION?

CHAPTER ONE

EXPLORING ADVICE AND GUIDANCE

You might be tired of hearing advice about managing your unmanageable feelings. Like I've said, a lot of advice isn't useful.

In your saddest or darkest moments, the words you have probably heard most from others might be something like *time heals everything*. Or maybe, *you'll feel better tomorrow*. Even if these old sayings tend to be true—sometimes, but not always—it might feel like these words trivialize your feelings into something you can just get over eventually.

What if that feeling lingers on, or goes away for a bit but comes back again? What about when time isn't a cure?

Then there's the complete nonadvice that masquerades as helpful advice. *You'll be fine. Cheer up. You're too young to be depressed. When I was your age, we had it much harder than you.* It's not surprising that many teenagers experiencing depression struggle to reach out when they are left feeling unsupported, isolated, dismissed, and even angry.

Many know this vicious cycle all too well. Feeling let down keeps us in our little worlds, just us and our disappointment and our depression. Venturing to reach outside that contained space of sadness and hurt is hard.

Humans are complex. What may feel like dismissal on your end might be what they think is support on their end. It's worth considering that most advice emerges from a well-meaning place.

When we see people whom we care about experiencing distress, usually, we want to help. A "just trying to be helpful" way of thinking, however, can dismiss or undermine very valid fears and feelings. You probably know what I mean by this already. Advice from others can put pressure on you to feel like you need to feel better in a hurry or hide your pain when you don't.

If you're feeling depressed, being told to try all these different solutions (or to sit and wait for time to work its allegedly magic healing powers) can be overwhelming and, well, depressing.

Most advice is too simple because—to be honest—we *want* solutions to be simple. Acknowledging others' suffering often makes us flawed humans feel uncomfortable, so we fix the source of our discomfort by believing our loved ones' hurts have simple causes and easy resolutions.

Some people do have a talent for listening without judgment, lending a peaceful presence instead of pressuring you to do things, or be there to offer you a plate of good food when everything seems gray. If you find them, give them some good food in return.

I'd be lying if I said it was easy to hear other people's problems without wanting to solve them or offer some far-too-simple solution. Even as a person with depression, I want to dish out advice sometimes when I know what I have to say oversimplifies things.

It gets better, I want to say—because it does. I know this simple truth.

I know the slog of trying to untie depression's tangled knots— underwater, in slow motion—is represented so inadequately in three simple words. There is no sentence in the world, in any language, quite full enough to offer adequate advice. I say it gets better, but what I mean is, it's complicated. So much goes into healing. I hope you can take the advice others offer not as solutions, but as signs that others want to give you healing.

Your family, friends, teachers, and others might have a natural human impulse for advising. This doesn't mean you don't have a support system. It means you do. If others are responding with their words of advice, however unhelpful, they're trying in their way to reach out and help. It's hard to feel helpless when a loved one is hurting, and advice seems like all we can give sometimes.

They're still your support system; they need a little guidance (not advice!) on how to be what you need. Reach out to family and friends and tell them what would be helpful from them. Maybe you want someone to agree that what happened to you that day was terrible, not for them to advise you how to tape your day and your mood back together.

Building your support system with a therapist or counselor is helpful. Contrary to common belief, most therapists and counselors don't give advice. Giving advice is *not even their job*. (The first time I heard this, my mind was blown.)

It is not part of therapists' job description to tell their clients what to think, what's right, how to live, or what to do. Therapy is designed to help you long term, so its goals are to guide you to making your realizations, not tell you what you should or should not do.

If you always have someone telling you what choice to make, the first time you have to make a significant choice on your own might be paralyzing and traumatic. You're unlikely to feel empowered or confident about making that choice. From the first time you're allowed to pick out your outfit or decide what you want to eat, you're learning how to function in a world of choices—and practice makes perfect. If a therapist makes those choices for you by telling you what you should do (or not do, as the case may be), you won't be practicing and growing.

What therapists *are* there for is to help you see your range of choices and help you think through your solutions more effectively. They can help you put skills in your emotional toolbox, teaching you coping strategies or techniques for evaluating and responding to problems.

For this reason, that's why this book focuses on that tenet of therapy. It aims to share anecdotes instead of giving advice.

I hope you feel empowered and seen when you read some of these anecdotes. Ultimately, the goal of these real experiences is to trust that you will hear what is useful to you and take what you need—whether that is a sense that you are not alone or modeling strategies you find helpful.

There is no one right way to tackle depression, and there is no one right way to read and use this book. While designed to address depression in teenagers, this book isn't just for people who have depression.

Even for readers who don't have depression, you might still be interested in understanding some of these processes to be more mindful of your thoughts and behaviors, as well as to develop better coping strategies. Everyone can benefit from adding a few more skills to your emotional toolbox.

In addition to being guided by anecdotes, this book addresses the role our minds and bodies play in our health and ability to cope with any difficulties we encounter. Understanding is sometimes a game changer. Even if nothing else in your life changes, but you understand the why of your body's physical and mental processes, there can be some relief.

CHAPTER TWO

EXPLORING DEPRESSION

One reason it can be easy for others to dish out advice without seeming to understand your particular feelings is that everyone has felt down at one time or another.

After all, depressed moods are healthy and appropriate responses to life's varied difficulties. (Another little human weakness is that it's in our nature to feel expertise at having experienced or done something—even just once—which is why people can think they're an expert suddenly when it comes to advising about feeling depressed.) The duration and severity of that mood vary depending on the situation, from an awkward social moment to feeling bored in school to grieving a loved one.

In these circumstances, there's an identifiable cause, experience, or event provoking your mood. There can be something reassuring about knowing *why* you feel your distress, however paradoxical that may sound.

Feeling depressed and having depression are rooted in the same emotional states and sensations, but a *depressed mood* is not the same as having *depression*. A depressed mood is only one part of depression's complicated web.

The distinction between the two is important to make. Before we can dive into more about depression's challenges and coping with them, we have to identify what depression means, as well as how its thought patterns and behaviors look. Doctors and therapists use guidelines covering a range of signs to distinguish a depressed mood from depression.

Don't dismiss your depression even if it seems mild or seems to have no cause. Depression wears many faces and moods. Check the myths about depression here. *Illustration by Christie Cognevich*

First, the guidelines aren't about severity. Having depression doesn't mean that you feel *worse* than "just" feeling down. It means the duration of these feelings (and the behaviors associated with those negative feelings, like over- or undereating when distressed, for example) have lasted two weeks or longer. This duration has also problematically impacted your everyday functioning.

Second, while we toss around words like "depression" as feelings of tremendous sadness, depression wears lots of different emotional faces. That means it can also manifest as frequent feelings of anger, annoyance, or feeling overwhelmed with stress. It can even feel like boredom, numbness, or emptiness. Depression can feel like too much feeling or no feeling at all.

And last, while depression can have a clear cause, it can also just as frequently emerge as if from nowhere. You don't need a reason to feel depressed. You can still have depression without a clear cause. And even if the initial cause is clear, depression can continue to linger. Either way, what might have started as a mood is now a problem.

If you're reading this book, you might be already familiar with the ugly shapes these problems can take. Difficulties with your family, friends, schoolwork, and just getting up and doing anything can feel like a chore or an exhausting task. Dreams for the future seem bleak or unattainable when *today* is impossible. After all, it's hard to function in your daily demands or find joy in anything when you feel bound in an intricate web of sadness, irritability, anger, disinterest, hopelessness, worthlessness, guilt, shame, or some tangled and unmanageable combination of all of these and more.

If you feel this way or have felt this way often, your depression could be more than a depressed mood. If you think your depressed moods don't last very long or rarely last past their causes, you might not have depression, or it might be very mild. Keep reading—building your emotional intelligence and coping strategies also gives you a good foundation for avoiding depression later on.

What do you realize now when you look back on discovering you had/have depression?

Emma

I compared myself to others a lot. Looking at everyone else, I never felt like my problems were serious enough to merit the depth of my pain. I heard it from my stepdad too: you don't know what *real* problems are. I definitely had a lot of compassion for others who were hurting; I didn't feel like I had a real reason myself.

In my junior year of high school, I took this creative writing class. I remember one time we were reading our work out loud for the class, and at that moment, I felt like an emotional fraud. One girl wrote about her mom dying young from cancer, and another wrote about how her dad had just died. It seemed like they had a right to carry that huge sadness and put it in their writing. I respected them for just writing about their fears and not being too afraid to spill it in front of everyone else. I just felt fake about it.

But after I saw that, I did start to put a little more of myself in my writing. Not autobiographical stuff, but I let some of my secret darkness creep into the emotional tone little by little. I felt kind of brave and embarrassed at the same time. I told myself to *get over it; you're writing stupid, dramatic, depressing things. You look like you want attention.* But no one else said anything negative about the stuff I was writing—they all seemed to appreciate it. That helped.

I think it took sharing a little bit of the pieces of myself I kept hidden from everybody to see that I did have depression, and I needed to acknowledge it to do anything about it.

Leila

I cried a lot all through high school. I constantly felt like a failure. You could say I was depressed, but I never sought help because I didn't think my life was bad enough to be diagnosed as depressed.

Nothing helped me, but I told myself, *That's life, you have to keep going.* I'd be damned if I ever acted like anything was wrong in front of anyone. I picked my head up and kept going because I felt no one was going to hold my hand through life.

Looking back now, I wish I could tell my younger self that seeking help is okay. Put your pride aside.

Charlie

I thought I was just having a hard time coping with skipping a grade. I moved from fifth directly to seventh grade. My old friends felt abandoned, and most slipped away. My new classmates weren't eager to make me feel included. They all knew each other already and were bonded in a way, so I was the outsider. I didn't realize what a huge deal it was to be a year younger than everyone else. I went from being confident to curling up inside of myself and going quiet.

My mom often came and ate lunch with me in the cafeteria at school, and she had a really fun, extroverted personality. Usually, I was on my own, but when she visited, quite a few other kids would join us. They'd say how they wished their parents would do that with them. That didn't make them my friends when she wasn't around.

It got worse when I went to high school, and now all of my old friends were still at a different school, and it would be weird

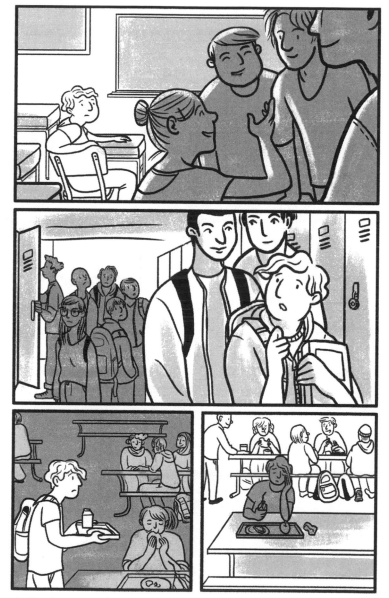

Charlie skipped a grade and struggled to connect with his new classmates.
Illustration by Kate Haberer

for my mom to eat there. I felt isolated a lot. It went on for a long time before I realized I wasn't just having a hard time coping. I was depressed.

Austin

I will never forget this as a kid. Everyone called me lazy. Saying, "He's lazy. He likes to stay in his room and watch movies all day."

I believed them for the longest time because of my weight. I thought because I was a little overweight as a kid, I was like, *Oh, I must be lazy.*

But then I thought, *No, I'm not lazy. But I don't have an artistic outlet, so my artistic outlet is watching the movies.* That was when I felt like I didn't fit in for sure.

How did I get through being alone? I've always been a big fan of movies. I used to watch movies and entertainers, and they're the people who I have to thank for that. They got me through.

I was struggling with depression and weight issues at that time. Thankfully, I was doing school theater shows, so that got me through, and I think looking towards the future has got me through a lot. Looking towards the future and seeing that there is a light at the end of the tunnel.

MORE THAN A MOOD

Depression tells lies.

This truth can be hard to process, because that depression is right there, lying about it telling lies.

Stretchy face filters, curved mirror effects, and face swaps on photo apps can have hysterical results. Despite the sometimes unexpected results, we feel in control, knowing they aren't accurate reflections of reality.

What if you had that filter inside your head showing an uglier version of your life? If your depressed mood lifts, you might be able to see the lies your mood told with clarity. If you have depression that lingers, you can get stuck in the lies.

There is no shame in experiencing serious pain, but long term, that hidden fun-house mirror can take your hurting thoughts and show them to you stretched, pinched, and otherwise distorted into profound hopelessness.

Moments of depression empty the wonder from the world, bleach joy into nothing. Your excitement for hobbies, activities, and sources of pleasure drains away into meaninglessness. What used to feel good doesn't anymore, and you start to doubt that it ever did feel good. Depression can tell you that you're a drag on your friends and family when you aren't, or that no one would care if you were gone. It can tell you that you have no purpose or point in this world and that feeling this way means you're broken. These are only a few of the ways that depression tells us endless lies.

Depression lies so expertly, and its lies look like truth. (Maybe because it hits us where our fears are, where we're vulnerable. It's easy to believe what we secretly fear.)

Many of us have no idea that depression's fun-house filter is telling lies about our selves, experiences, surroundings, and even our thoughts. Depression says our feelings control us, but also, they're our fault. It claims our past joys weren't even real to begin with, or if they were, we would never be that happy again. It tells us it is "just a mood," asks us why can't we *just get over it*—while also whispering that we will never feel any better. In this way, depression repaints both our past *and* our future with its shadows.

When others dismiss depression as merely a bad mood, an adolescent phase to outgrow, something that is cliché in teens, or even an unwillingness on your part to deal with your problems, they reinforce (however accidentally) the lies of depression's ugly filter. How can we *not* believe what we hear not only from our family, friends, and peers but also from inside our heads?

One of depression's biggest weapons against us is the unwarranted shame and stigma so many feel. If you feel ashamed, you are unlikely to speak up or reach out. Boosting the conversation surrounding depression and other mental health issues, however, decreases stigma. Depression has never been something to whisper about, and the advent of internet communities and social media have helped drag it out of its shadows into the light.

Everything looks different in the bright light with no filter. It's hard dragging the dark fun-house mirror out of its confusing reflective maze into a place where you can see depression's smoke and mirrors keeping you trapped in your head. It starts by accepting that you are more than your emotions and your fears. You are more than the ways you think you're not good enough or the ways others have let you down. These feelings aren't permanent flaws or something that you were meant to suffer. You are more than the lies depression whispers to you.

Your feelings are valid. If you are experiencing depression, it is more than a mood.

Worlds of difference exist between knowing something on a surface level and taking that knowledge inside of you to feel it internally. You might already know depression is lying to you but don't fully believe it yet.

You don't have to be there yet. You're getting there. It is a process.

Did you ever get in your own way when it came to getting help?

Emma

I know now that it didn't help my depression that I was making myself carry a ton of weird guilt, thinking others had it worse. Feelings aren't a competition. Probably the first step for me with coping was acknowledging that I was allowed to be depressed.

It sounds stupid when I say it out loud: "You're allowed to feel depressed." But I think a lot of people are like me in thinking they don't have the right to feel as badly as they do.

I'm my first support system, so I have to listen to my body and mind when it says something is wrong instead of telling myself to shut up.

Charlie

I knew my mom supported me no matter what, but I also knew that she struggled with depression. I always said I was okay, and things were getting better because I didn't want to be a burden on her.

Audrey

For a long time, I prided myself on "not being affected" by emotions. That gave me more time to concentrate on work and school, I said. It made me smarter, more rational, I said. But truthfully, I was being affected by my emotions, but since I couldn't name them, I wasn't aware of how damaging they were. I couldn't sit with them, understand them, and work with them to make conscious and healthy decisions about my life.

In fairness, I had many therapists tell me this, but I was smarter than them. How could the fact my family didn't talk about feelings have anything to do with how I couldn't acknowledge my feelings? No, I was just born with all this inner turmoil; this is just the way I am and always will be.

It wasn't until my *second* inpatient stay at a psychiatric hospital I began to take my condition not only seriously but also consider it as something treatable.

WHAT ARE THE WARNING SIGNS OF DEPRESSION?

Depression's stereotypical image is moping or crying all the time, and while that can signal depression, there are a lot of other emotions and behaviors that are warning signs.

Beyond having a depressed mood or feeling troubled, the specific list of depression's warning signs will vary slightly according to which guidelines your country follows, but these guidelines are nearly identical. In the United States, a manual called the *Diagnostic and Statistical Manual of Mental Disorders* (often referred to as the *DSM*) published by the American Psychiatric Association determines the diagnostic criteria for depression. In the United Kingdom and many other countries, the World Health Organization's *International Classification of Diseases* sets the criteria, which isn't a precise checklist. You will not fit every sign perfectly; some will match, and some won't.

The equation for a diagnosis combines a series of factors: your feelings and behaviors, the length of time you've been experiencing them, and the negative effect these feelings and behaviors have on your life.

If your depressed mood lasts for more than two weeks and is compounded by boredom, disinterest, or a bleak sense that nothing is worthwhile (not even your previous pursuits and interests), you might have depression. In addition to a persistent depressed mood and lack of pleasure and interest, the primary signs your doctor or therapist will look for include:[1]

- Changes in eating habits

- Changes in sleeping habits

- Decreased activity or fatigue after a minor effort

- Increased irritability or anger

- Plans or acts of self-harm or suicide

- Hopelessness

- Low self-esteem, feelings of worthlessness

- Difficulty with concentration or making decisions

- Excessive guilt, shame

Remember, there are always individual variations in how your body and mind manifest depression. You don't need to have every single one of these signs—and these aren't necessarily the *only* signs of depression—but to provide an accurate diagnosis, your specialist will be looking for a combination of these affecting your functioning. Other secondary signs they will take into consideration include:

- Feeling helpless to change your feelings or circumstances

- Boredom, disinterest

- Physical issues (headaches, stomachaches, other discomforts)

- Difficulty coping with life events

- Isolation

- Feeling distracted or forgetful

- Frequent absences from school or usual activities

- Reckless choices, alcohol or substance abuse

- Perfectionism, critical self-evaluation

Maybe you do recognize some of these feelings and behaviors in yourself. Now, what should you do?

Talk to someone if you recognize some of these signs to get support and additional care.

Regardless of whether it turns out that you have depression, another mental health issue, or are simply going through normal life, having struggles, thoughts, and emotions that are bothering you are reasons to reach out. (Yes, this means that nearly everyone should be reaching out throughout their lives!)

How did you recognize your depression? Did others recognize it?

Emma

What did my depression look like on the outside? I know one reason my depression wasn't diagnosed until many years later was that I was so functional. Inside, I felt dead and broken and bleeding all the time. On the outside, I was just this smiling, masked version of myself who got up, went to school, did the things.

After getting a diagnosis—which I'd lived in perpetual terror of and then turned out to be relieved to get—my parents said they'd had no idea anything was going on with me.

"I *know*," I said. "That was the point. I worked hard to make sure no one knew."

But deep down, I knew because of the effort that I'd had to put forth to keep the smile going and keep the outside looking fine that the inside wasn't doing so great. I collapsed into bed every night, exhausted by the effort of performing myself every night. I knew inside how tired my body was and how exhausted my mind was of dragging around all my thoughts all the time.

Charlie

For the longest time, I thought I was just more shy than I already knew. Two distinct memories from that time when I realized these were red flags that I was very depressed:

One, I was taking a pan of tater tots out of the oven, and my brother laughed loudly and crazily, startling me into dropping the pan on the floor. I immediately deteriorated into tears. Even after my brother apologized profusely and helped me clean up the mess, it took a long time for me to pull myself together.

And two, I was an artistic kid, so I had lots of art supplies. One day I was just spaced out at my desk, staring at my box of razor blades, fantasizing about killing myself. They were so sharp . . . it would be so easy. I did this rather often.

That's how I realized I was depressed, and I needed help.

WHAT DOES DEPRESSION LOOK LIKE IN ACTION?

If we think about depression as more than a mood, then it makes more sense that you can be depressed regardless of a range of moods—even good ones.

As a result, depression doesn't look the same for everyone, or even the same for you from day to day. Because these signs and symptoms can vary widely, teenage depression often goes undiagnosed and untreated—only half who experience depression will be diagnosed before adulthood. On average, it takes about *eleven years* between the emergence of mental health symptoms and beginning treatment—especially if you are younger when your symptoms emerge.[2] You deserve better than that. If you're reading this book, you're already way ahead of the game.

First, try to keep an eye on *your* "normal," your baseline, a starting point from which we can measure variation across experiences, states of mind, and moods. Like there is no one-size-fits-all advice, there are no one-size-fits-all checklists for feeling normal. Not everyone has the same "normal," so what you can look for is *shifts* in your habits, patterns, feelings, and activities to establish where you usually are and where you are when you're low.

Observe changes. If you like to go for morning runs to clear your head, and you start sleeping late and skipping it, that's a change to note. If being around people often drains your emotional batteries, then you probably aren't into big social activities. Feeling exhausted by and avoiding group activities wouldn't necessarily be a symptom of depression. If you did value one-on-one interactions with a close friend and you find yourself now avoiding those moments, however, allow yourself to explore those feelings a little closer. There's nothing wrong with needing space sometimes, but are you in need of some temporary space, or are you curling up into yourself and away from your support system? The difference can be subtle but important.

You know your mind and body best. Even if others think you're perfectly happy, you might be so convincing at going through the motions and keeping a smile on your face that no one would ever know anything was wrong. But inside, you might have started to feel joyless or numb. Even if no one else notices any changes in you, if you feel like your mental state isn't in a good place, take notice.

Second, while depression doesn't need triggers, pay attention to changes, events, and stressors, which can affect your emotional equilibrium. You can do this by paying attention to your body at peace and then during stressful times. Where do you feel it when you're overwhelmed, embarrassed, or sad? Where do you feel it when you are calm, happy, or excited? Where do you feel your tiredness? Pain and fatigue are your body's way of speaking to you. Being aware of constant fatigue or pain can be an external clue to internal states.

Regularly checking in with yourself can help you start to identify the turning points where your mind-set starts slipping from positive to negative, or your body starts shifting from comfortable to uncomfortable. Are there people who regularly put you at ease or people who make you feel unhappy after interacting with them? Which situations relax you, and which situations tense you? It's only in identifying your body's signals that you can act on them. If there are toxic situations or people you have to endure for various reasons, you can keep aware of their impact on you and prepare your coping methods in advance.

When you compare your "normal" to your current state, does anything feel different? When you check in with yourself, are you more regularly feeling "off" from your normal physical and mental state? Keep track of these times. Are they linked to certain activities, certain people? Where were you in your life and your head when something changed?

The increasing awareness of mental health struggles means there are a growing number of mindfulness journals and mental health trackers available to fit your needs and interests.

Searching online for mood trackers or mood journaling activities can help you find a good fit for you that doesn't feel like a chore to fill out—there is a wide variety available online to download or to model in your journal. There are also mood trackers available on the author's website for free (https://www.christiecognevich.com/downloads).

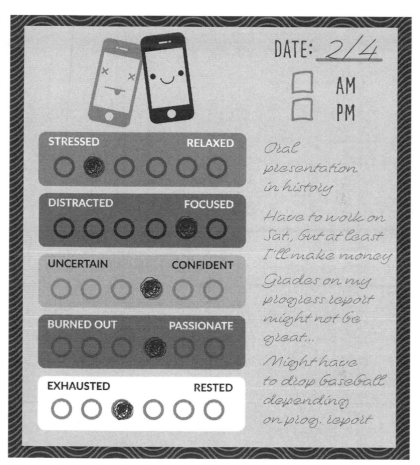

This sample mood tracker shows how filling it out can help reveal patterns in your activities, interactions, and emotions. Because depression can affect memory and functioning, it can be hard to see how your mood is affected by your experiences, but trackers can help document this over time. Download a free blank version for you to use on the author's website at christiecognevich .com. *Illustration by Christie Cognevich*

These trackers are useful because emotional awareness is a big first step for several healthier life habits—and something as seemingly "simple" as knowing what you feel when you feel it isn't always as easy as it sounds.

DATE

3/16

MOOD

||||||||||||||||||||||||||

TODAY'S LYRIC

*But look at where
I ended up, I'm all
good already*

TODAY'S SONG

*"Don't Start
Now" - Dua
Lipa*

IDEAS

*Watercolor video.
Painting for each
song verse and have
different people hold
them up*

ACTIVITIES

*Art portfolio
Multimedia
video idea
Coffee with Sam?*

Mood trackers like this one can help determine patterns in your activities, interactions, and emotions. Download a free blank version for you to use on the author's website at christiecognevich.com. *Illustration by Christie Cognevich*

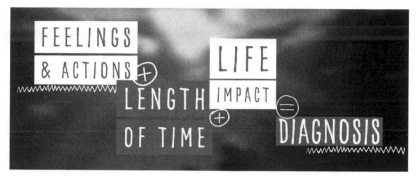

Everyone's depression looks different, so this is the straightforward formula a mental health professional uses to determine a formal depression diagnosis. *Illustration by Christie Cognevich*

DIAGNOSIS

Do you have any strategies for knowing when you're feeling "normal" or not?

Jael

My therapist introduced me to journaling to help me pay attention to my mind and body. It's not like a traditional "dear diary" kind of journal, but just a way to jot down a few quick things about my state of mind and activity. At first, my therapist gave me printouts for me to follow, but now I do my journal in a regular notebook.

It's not anything too personal, either, if someone finds it. It'll just say something like, "Upbeat, took a nap, worked on an essay, productive," and maybe I'll write down the name of the playlist I used when working on that essay that helped me be productive. If it's a rough day, it'll say, "No motivation, *Great British Bake Off* marathon on Netflix, made tacos after, didn't finish homework."

When I'm depressed, the last thing I'm doing is paying attention to my moods and thought patterns and habits. I like to be involved in a lot of activities, but I also have a tipping point where I either overinvolve myself as a distraction from my problems, or

I drop everything for Netflix marathons and get nothing done. I never actually noticed I have these turning points until I started tracking it.

Something that also surprised me is that my moods cycle intensely throughout the month. Not to be cliché—I hate when guys ask if a woman is on her period when she's moody—but it was only through journaling that I realized when I'm about to have my period, I become the most miserable, depressed person on the planet. It's not during my period itself, it's just a couple days before-hand, but I feel dark.

With the journaling, I find that I can be a little bit more pre-pared. I've even thought about scheduling a "danger zone" alarm on my phone calendar as a joke to remind myself. I haven't yet.

CHAPTER THREE

TAKING THE FIRST STEPS TO HEALING

R each out.
The person you talk to can be any adult you feel most comfortable with, including family, friends, teachers, coaches, counselors, or religious leaders. If you're worried that your parents won't be supportive, this adult can help you come up with strategies to work with your parents or serve as a positive intermediary.

If you don't have an adult who you think is available to talk to on this list—or you don't feel comfortable reaching out to someone you know in person—there are many resources for nonjudgmental, helpful people available both online and on the phone to help support you in finding someone you *can* talk to.

If you think you have a few signs of depression or your symptoms are very mild, you might not need a doctor or therapist. Everyone can benefit from better mental health, whether they have a diagnosis or not, however, and communication helps build support systems. Keep talking. Keep reaching out.

If you *do* recognize many symptoms of depression in yourself, try to notice your mental barriers as a first step to lowering them. You aren't alone if you feel reluctant.

Reaching out is easier said than done, of course. Humans are good at talking themselves out of getting support for a million reasons—especially when we need it most. We're good at paralyzing ourselves. Maybe we think that we only have *some* of these warning signs, but not enough. Maybe we tell ourselves we have no one to trust, that no one cares, or that we're making a big deal over nothing. Maybe we worry that we're making too much trouble for our loved ones, and we put their needs first over ours. Maybe we feel angry and let down at the world because we've tried to get help in our ways, and no one has helped. Maybe we're just scared. All of these things are normal and reasonable.

But you will have to lower these mental barriers to create change. Thoughts and fears are just that: thoughts and fears. When they get stuck on a loop, they can feel like all we have inside, but there's more to you than that repeating negative thought pattern.

To break a repeating loop, change your step to throw the whole loop off. It's like a dance. One different step and the dance partner (in this case, your thoughts) shifts a little in response.

Make yourself a playlist of songs that make you feel strong or motivated and listen to it before talking to someone—focus just on the words or the sound to quiet the persistent thoughts in your mind. Wear your exterior armor—your favorite shirt or hat or the big jacket or the cool boots or your signature makeup that puts a little more fire in your heart. Let the physical transformation seep into your mental pattern. Talk to a friend and ask if they'll go with you to talk to an adult and ask them to distract you from your looping thoughts.

Next, communicate with an adult. Talk honestly about how you've been feeling. The hardest part of this whole process is almost certainly the part where you reach out and talk to someone with the intent of getting help. It is highly likely that others might recognize that you are struggling in some way; it is much less likely that they understand how much or in what ways you are struggling.

Be clear that you need help getting to a doctor or mental health specialist, including secondary support—like if you have health insurance benefits, you might need assistance navigating what the benefits cover and which providers you can see. You may even need help from that adult to guide you in working with your parents to get the support and care you need.

You may not know just yet how you want to phrase what you say. Having a script prepared in advance is useful; it doesn't have to come out perfectly. Doing this as soon as possible means less wait time between reaching out and seeing a doctor or therapist.

- Convey the seriousness of how you have been feeling—especially if you have thoughts that worry you or scare you.

- Ask if they can help you find more resources and get an appointment with a specialist, or even accompany you to talk to the doctor.

- If you are in immediate crisis, ask for help in getting to an emergency room or help to call 911 (or your country's emergency number) or a suicide prevention hotline if you don't feel able.

Keep talking in the meantime—not just to adults but to your whole support system. You may have to wait a little bit to see someone after reaching out. This gap of time is incredibly important in keeping you feeling safe and supported. There are options not only for talking with people in person but finding online support as well.

- Spend quality time with people you can trust who listen and make you feel supported—surround yourself with the people you love and trust.

- Have honest conversations about your feelings and your needs.

- Embrace your hobbies and other activities you love even if they don't seem as fulfilling right now.

- Get help making a safety plan (there will be more on this later in the book).

- Talk to others in online communities where you feel safe.

The process is listed as simple steps, but the steps are not easy. It's okay if some steps feel difficult. If you feel overwhelmed, try approaching a single step instead of looking ahead to what might come next week or the week after. When you hear a lot of people telling you to think about your future, it may sound difficult, but your future is built one day at a time.

Remember, if you or a loved one is facing a mental health emergency, including thinking about suicide or self-harm, call one of the helplines listed below or go to the emergency room immediately.

Even if you feel hopeless to do anything or don't know what to do, others do know what to do. Just pause, breathe, and reach out right away to one of the resources listed here. There are many safe, confidential, free, immediate options available for you to talk, text, or chat with someone if you are in crisis.

- **In the United States**, call 911 for an emergency or the 24/7 National Suicide Prevention Hotline at 1-800-273-8255. There are options for Spanish speakers and the deaf or hard of hearing. If you feel more comfortable texting, the Crisis Text Line is a free 24/7 text message service for people in crisis. Text HOME to 741741.

- **In the United Kingdom**, call 999 for an emergency or the National Health Services' First Response Service for mental health at 111, Option 2. If you feel more comfortable texting, Shout is a free 24/7 text message service for people in crisis. Text SHOUT to 85258.

- **In Canada**, call 911 for an emergency or the 24/7 Kids Help phone service (anyone under the age of twenty) at 1-800-668-6868 or Crisis Services Canada (no age restriction) at 1-833-456-4566. Quebec residents can call Crisis Services at 1-866-277-3553. If you feel more comfortable texting, the Crisis Text Line is a free 24/7 text message service for people in crisis. Text CONNECT (for English) or PARLER (for French) to 686868.

- **In Australia**, call 000 for an emergency or the 24/7 Kids Helpline phone service (anyone under the age of twenty-five) at 1800 55 1800 or Lifeline (no age restriction) at 13 11 14. Both Lifeline (https://www.lifeline.org.au/) and Kids Helpline (https://www.kidshelpline.com.au/) have online chat features available at their websites.

What was the turning point that made you reach out for help?

Emma

It's an understatement to say I found it hard to get help.

I was a perfectionist, really hard on myself, always convinced I wasn't good enough. I felt so miserable for so long. Eventually, I felt sick all the time. I started skipping classes and struggling to convince myself there was even a reason to get out of bed in the morning. That started me on this impossible cycle of hating myself for having a hard time, which made things harder, which started the whole cycle again. I never talked to anyone; I just said I was sick and kept missing school. That probably went on for years without me saying anything about how I was feeling.

My boyfriend broke up with me. We'd been friends since we were young, and I thought we'd be together through thick and thin. He was a charming extrovert. I was a quiet introvert, but we just went together.

We were still messaging back and forth for a few weeks. I felt devastated, but I thought it was just a temporary break. But one day we wrapped up our conversation, and I told him that I loved him and he didn't text it back. Just silence. It was the worst feeling.

I'm sure a lot of people will find it dramatic when I say it felt literally like a lightning bolt of pain shooting through my chest, but that's what I felt at that moment. It felt dramatic at the time.

I got up and just started walking. I felt everything too hard and sharp and also really hollow inside. I didn't know how to make sense of that in my head, either.

I remember it pretty well. A gray sky kind of day where it was drizzling off and on with a few minutes of real rain every so often before going back to just damp and dreary. I didn't know where I was going, but I walked past the cafeteria, which had this glass wall, and I could see everyone inside. It made me feel alone. I wasn't a part of that world at all, everyone warm inside with bright colors with me outside, alone, in the gray. At the time, I remember that felt symbolic, like confirming what I'd always thought, that I wasn't good enough and didn't belong and all of my fears that I'd never be happy.

After her boyfriend broke up with her, Emma went for a walk to clear her head, and found herself walking into the counselor's office for help.
Illustration by Kate Haberer

I just wandered outside, feeling blank for a little bit. That was my tipping point. I could have just gone home and gotten in my bed like I wanted to and go to sleep. Or I could talk to someone.

I went sort of blank and autopiloted over to the counselor's office. I don't remember what I said to the person at the front desk, but she gave me this survey about various habits and feelings I might have had. It was so much easier to check boxes and be honest and stop feeling cold and empty inside.

There was something so relieving by being honest with the questionnaire. How often did I feel anxious, worried, or scared about things in my life? All the time! How often did I have trouble sleeping because my mind wouldn't stop thinking? Often! How often did I feel like my sadness was overtaking my life? Constantly!

I guess filling out the questionnaire made me feel seen. It wasn't good news; the checklist was showing I was depressed and anxious, but it was just a huge sigh of relief that I was in the right place to feel what I was feeling.

It's a long story, but that was the very start of doing what I needed to do for myself to finally start feeling better.

Elise

I realized that I was genuinely suicidal when I was fourteen after I started a new school, and all of my old friends ditched me. I don't know if I wanted to die permanently, but I did want to die right then. I didn't want to have to live anymore.

I think the thing that saved me was because even though I didn't want to live at that moment, I was curious to see what might come next, that maybe there would be a different future around the corner. That's why I told my parents.

When I finally told them, they both cried. I didn't want to go to therapy and told my parents that if they made me, I would lie to the therapist. I promised to make up all sorts of stuff and make the therapist think I was crazy.

But—somehow—they found me a funny therapist, and he gets my sense of humor. Talking with him is great.

WHAT IF I DON'T HAVE
MONEY OR SUPPORT?

You may not feel like you can afford treatment, or your family is against therapy. What can you do if you are in an unsupportive or dangerous situation, or you are unable to talk to a safe, nonjudgmental adult to get help? What can you do if you don't feel like you have access to mental health care?

You are not without help, and there are resources and options designed especially for people without easy access to them.

In the United States (211.org) and Canada (211.ca), 211 is a free and confidential resource to help people of all ages find free or low-cost support and services. You can call 211 if you need to talk, need to find support for your mental health, or if you need help getting out of a dangerous or abusive household or relationship.

Many licensed counselors and therapists set aside a few patient slots for free "pro bono" services as part of their ethical obligation to provide better mental health to everyone, not just the economically privileged. In addition to using 211 to potentially locate pro bono services, try looking online for local therapists who might be a good fit and inquire if they have any pro bono slots available—you might have to explain your situation in brief, but remember that they are confidential even if you don't end up working with them. Many more offer services on a "sliding scale," which means while it might not be free, they adjust the cost of their services lower to fit your ability to pay.

There are many free support groups out there for a variety of issues, interests, and identities. The National Alliance on Mental Illness (nami. org) is a good place to begin looking. Remember that local libraries, universities, and places of worship also offer many community resources and support groups and can even guide you to find funding to get the help you need. You may find that you feel most comfortable in a support group that isn't necessarily mental health focused but instead gives you a community based on your interests and hobbies. Seek out groups where you feel safe to build a support system around yourself.

Last, you do not have to be in an immediate state of crisis to contact any of the mental health hotlines already listed. If you feel like you need to talk to someone no matter how big or small the issue, they are there every day. Hotline counselors are incredibly valuable if you can't get a therapy appointment quickly enough or can't afford one right now.

What did you do when you didn't have support at home for your mental health?

Emma

We were poor, I didn't have health insurance, and probably the biggest reason I was struggling with depression for so many years was because of my stepdad's abuse all through my childhood. So I didn't exactly feel safe saying to my stepdad, "Hey, I need to talk to someone about what's going on at home!"

I was pretty close to rock bottom when I found out that pro bono counseling was a thing, which I still think is a very cool concept. I found a licensed counselor who volunteered an hour a week to see pro bono patients. I was able to work with her for free for a year, and over that year, she helped me to get out of the abusive situation and testify against my stepfather in court. It was terrifying to testify, and I still had a long way to go with my depression, but she helped me so much. I couldn't have done it otherwise.

I kept seeing her after the pro bono year because there was a state fund for victims of crime that paid for another year of my therapy.

If you don't have any luck with the first few counselors not doing pro bono work or not having any open slots, keep looking. Don't feel weird about asking if they offer any pro bono services. I can say that pro bono counseling saved my life.

Cailyn

The other day my mom came up to me and said, "Cailyn, I'm very worried about you. You don't eat, you don't sleep, and you sit in your room all the time. Are you doing drugs?"

I was like, "Really? Is that the answer? Is there any possibility that I'm depressed?" and she said, "I have depression. I know what depression looks like."

That was disappointing. And it doesn't work that way. Just because my symptoms aren't the same as hers, she thinks I'm not depressed.

So this year, I've been going to the school counselor, which surprised me that it helps. My experience has been that I'll go in there crying because there's something I thought was making me sad. We'll have a conversation, and I'll realize that it's something else. I like walking out feeling clearer.

It's been good to talk to the counselor since I can't confide in my parents with the kind of relationship we have.

WHY DOES GETTING A DIAGNOSIS MATTER?

If you recognize the signs of depression in yourself, the thought of going to a doctor, counselor, or other specialists may make you feel overwhelmed, angry, or afraid. If you already know how depressed you feel, why does it matter if someone else agrees? If you're not sure how you feel, it's reasonable to feel fear or anger about how a diagnosis might stick a label on you or say you're weak.

So why should you seek help from a specialist? Simple validation or getting labeled isn't the goal. A diagnosis is an incredibly useful starting point for figuring out more about your condition and specific needs. From this starting point, you can get treatment, knowledge, and resources to help your quality of living.

For some people, a small but essential part of receiving a diagnosis is the internal reassurance that your feelings aren't mysterious or impossible to pinpoint. A diagnosis puts a face and a name to a problem, and having a name for what you're experiencing can be a relief. After all, a condition is just a recognizable state of being that fits a pattern other people have too. Another related facet of this relief is that some feel a diagnosis reduces the sense of stigma. Knowing your mental state and behaviors make sense as part of that identifiable pattern of behavior can help *diminish* the feeling that you are alone, flawed, broken, or weak.

Even if having a diagnosis doesn't make a positive mental or emotional impact for you, it is also a necessary component of receiving health insurance coverage or, if you don't have health insurance, to qualify for other resources to help with your treatment.

However unexpected this may sound, a diagnosis for depression can improve your physical condition once you begin treatment or therapy. Mental and physical health are closely linked. We know that individuals with mental health issues suffer physically as well—this has been proven across the world in many studies. For example, people with depression have a 40 percent higher risk of developing cardiovascular and metabolic diseases than others.[1] The World Health Organization lists untreated depression as the top cause of poor health and disability worldwide.[2] Mental and physical illnesses often occur together, a situation doctors refer to as "comorbidity." Comorbidity means two or more conditions (whether mental or physical) happening at the same time, but having simultaneous conditions also means they can interact together to make you feel worse. Helping one can help the other.

With the help of a specialist, you can explore various options tailored to your diagnosis and build an individualized treatment plan. You may be doing some things on your own that are helping, but there are lots of options, both with medication and medication-free, depending on your needs. Your treatment plan might include some activities like attending individual or group counseling, finding support communities in person or online, identifying troublesome activities or relationships in your life, building a system of trusted individuals for emotional support, maintaining a log or journal to self-monitor moods and experiences, and developing a routine of activities that help you feel healthier and happier.

Did that list of activities make you feel exhausted or defeated just thinking about it? The benefit of a diagnosis is that you'll have support in guiding you through the next steps—you won't be on your own to tackle them.

How do you feel about saying you have depression?

Blake

I was in a group therapy session one time, and the counselor told us that language has power. According to him, saying, "I am sad" suggests that we're only what we feel. When you turn it around and say, "I feel sad" or "I have depression," it puts you back in control of your emotions. That way depression is just a feeling or condition, not your identity. It made sense, but at the same time, I don't think any of us in the session took it seriously.

Later, we did an activity where we wrote down things that hurt us and stomped on the paper (which, to be honest, felt good). After we did that, the counselor told us to write the name of someone special to us on another piece of paper. When he told us to ball up *that* paper and stomp all over it, none of us wanted to.

I was like, "What? I'm not going to stomp on my grandma!"

He laughed and said, "See? Words *do* have the power to affect your feelings."

It was funny, but he was right. That little piece of paper wasn't my grandma, but just putting her name on it changed how I felt about it—so now I say that I feel depressed instead of saying that I am depressed.

Charlie

When I was younger, I was very weird about saying I have depression. I felt like there was something wrong with me—like it meant I was crazy because it's like a clinical term. I thought if you have to see a counselor, that means you're crazy. My brother always said my mom was crazy, and I looked up to him. I didn't want to fail him in that way.

But now I encourage *everyone* to see a counselor. It's hugely, hugely helpful and that stigma needs to be gone.

Now I don't feel weird about saying I have depression. It's like saying I have brown hair. It's just something to have like anything else.

CHAPTER FOUR

LOOKING AT
THE NUMBERS

While no one shares the same experiences, thoughts, or reactions, teenagers with depression are not alone in their feelings—not just among immediate peers but internationally. Whether you know this yet or not, you share a community with many others who sometimes or often struggle with their emotions—a large community with an increasing voice finally receiving greater recognition around the globe. Millions of teenagers worldwide report having experienced a major depressive episode, often reporting struggling with extreme pressure to be attractive, fit in, and be successful. They report that their feelings of well-being generally center on their satisfaction with school life, parental relationships, and personal appearance.[1]

Shame makes silence, and silence makes isolation. But even if you do feel isolated or ashamed, the numbers reveal that many others are right there alongside you. You are not alone or the odd one out, a bittersweet reality. In most countries, life satisfaction levels for teenagers have decreased between 2015 and 2018, while over a quarter of teenagers in the UK report they are not satisfied with life.[2] In 2017, more than three million American teenagers reported recently experiencing depression, a figure 59 percent higher than a decade prior.[3] The same year, a large study revealed that at age fourteen, nearly a quarter of girls and one in ten boys in the United Kingdom reported struggling with depressive symptoms.[4] In Canada, approximately 5 percent of male and 12 percent of female adolescents have experienced a major depressive episode.

Adolescent depression's growing recognition destigmatizes mental health issues and encourages adults—politicians, doctors, parents, counselors—to provide better resources and support. Of course, these staggering numbers also reveal how much work human beings have left to do in tackling serious problems for vulnerable populations and even just supporting one another in general.

While teenagers are experiencing anxiety and depression in ever-increasing rates, they are also more clearly recognizing it among their peers as an issue and talking about it. Ninety-six percent of American teenagers across a broad income spectrum believe problems with anxiety and depression are issues they see in their peer community. Overall, 70 percent report that is a *major* problem among their peers, and only 4 percent feel it is not a problem. Anxiety and depression are some of the most pressing issues teens report, far outstripping bullying, drugs, alcohol, and poverty as concerns.[5]

- The adolescent brain is incredibly sensitive to stress and brain changes during adolescence, increasing teenage vulnerability to depression and anxiety. Mood disorders like depression nearly double from age thirteen to age eighteen, from 8.4 percent of thirteen-year-olds to 15.4 percent of eighteen-year-olds.[6]

- In both the United States and Canada, suicide is the second leading cause of death for adolescents ages ten through twenty-four.[7] In the United Kingdom, suicide is the leading cause of death for adolescents.[8]

- Over 70 percent of adolescents ages eighteen and under have struggled with feelings of loneliness.[9]

- At some point in their lives, anxiety affects 30 percent of children and adolescents, but 80 percent *never* get help. Only 1 percent of youth with anxiety seek treatment in the year symptoms begin, even though untreated anxiety disorders are linked to depression, school failure, and increased difficulty in transitioning into adulthood.[10]

- The average age of onset for social anxiety disorder is fourteen, and the untreated combination of depression and social anxiety is strongly associated with more depressive symptoms, including suicidal thoughts. With treatment, there are very high long-term success rates for recovery.[11]

PART II
COPING WITH DEPRESSION

CHAPTER FIVE

THE PROBLEM
WITH STRESS

There are many challenges and pressures you face in today's image-centric, goals-based world—all of these challenges are stressors. Teens are reporting ever-increasing stress rates, and unhealthy amounts of stress affect your daily mind-set and ability to function. Moments that feel stressful play a role in making you feel vulnerable, helpless, or in despair. In addressing these life challenges, this chapter explains some of the mental processes that cause these dark feelings and empowering ways to escape the mental habits that tell us we are helpless victims to life's suffering.

You won't—and shouldn't—feel calm, happy, or relaxed all the time. Avoiding all stress isn't the goal, because you need stress sometimes; however, feeling stressed all the time is dangerous. Because depression is affected by your brain chemistry, hormones, and thought patterns, your stress (which affects all three) can play a role in producing or worsening depressive symptoms.

Stress is an inevitable part of your daily life—and studies show that's true now more than ever. While some stress is normal, in a 2018 survey evaluating stress levels among young Americans ages fifteen to twenty-one, the American Psychological Association concluded that the United States' youngest generation is reporting the highest levels of stress and mental health concerns out of all its generations. Safety is a massive concern provoking adolescent stress—anxiety about mass shootings, school shootings, and sexual violence feature high on the list of stressors.[1] In a fast-paced, technology-based world like the one you live in—where you're always connected and always moving—stressors can keep you feeling under pressure and unable to enjoy your life.

Teenagers encounter enormous amounts of stress in their daily lives. It probably comes as little surprise to you that 83 percent of teenagers rate themselves as significantly or somewhat significantly stressed by school. In general, American teenagers rate themselves during the school year at higher stress levels (a 5.8 on a ten-point scale) than adults do (a 5.1 on the same scale). During the school year, over a quarter of these teenagers report experiencing extremely high levels of stress—rating their current stress at an eight or higher on a ten-point scale, far beyond the rating these teens suggest is healthy—no more than a 3.9 stress level on the ten-point scale. Far more teenagers report that their stress level has increased in the last year (31 percent) or that they feel their stress levels will increase in the coming year (34 percent) than those reporting a decrease in stress over the year (16 percent).[2]

However, understanding your stress can greatly help in gaining a sense of control over it.

What makes your stress worse?

Blake

I can't stand feeling like stress is a competition sometimes. It stresses me out! Whenever I'm with my friends, and we start venting, sometimes it feels like a game of who has the most to get done or the most problems or whose problems aren't real problems. Don't get me wrong; my friends can be amazing and supportive. I love being able to share what's going on with my friends without us trying to one-up each other. You know, saying, "Oh yeah, that's awful, but let me tell you what happened to *me*." That's not helpful.

I remember one time someone said—not to me, but our friend—"That's because your problems aren't real problems." That bothered me because no one knows some of the stuff we carry that we *don't* talk about, and what weighs nothing to me might be a much bigger deal for someone else.

And I know, at least for myself, that even if I look calm on the outside, I might be a mess on the inside. I think I hide my stress well. It's a "fake it till you make it" situation. I might be doing well in school and at my job, but I still cry myself to sleep every single night because I'm so overwhelmed. Sometimes I can't sleep because I make lists in my head over and over of things I need to do and not forget when I get stressed out. And then sometimes all I do is sleep because I'm so tired from everything I have to do that I can't even get up to do it.

In general, it's impossible to know who's super stressed and who's not and who's coping and who's not. It makes things worse for me to compare my stress to everyone else or to try to keep faking that I'm okay when I'm not.

Someone told me once that it's okay to drop your basket sometimes. I like that phrase. I think it captures how I feel when everyone is either showing off their baskets that are overloaded or everyone is trying to cover up their baskets and pretend like they're emptier than they are. I think it's important to keep a balance between the two to prevent my stress from getting worse. Be able to share honestly, don't hide, but also don't make it some weird game where the person whose life sucks worse wins.

Cailyn

Procrastination makes my stress so much worse. Most of the time during school, I feel like *I can do this, I'm ready!*

But then I go home and take a nap, and things pile up so much that I'm overwhelmed. Then I have to decide I'd rather fail *this* quiz than *that* test. I have to rationalize and prioritize what's going to matter the most to me. It's impossible to do it all.

I mean, I've tried to do it all—and it was *bad*. So I guess trying to do everything also makes my stress worse. There have been nights where I'd stay up all night—there was a phase I went through for junior year where I had so much going on. I was scared if I went to sleep I'd be too tired the next day, but if I could power through and stay awake, I could get through. There's a point where you get past the exhaustion, but that was a rough time. When I did sleep, the next morning, I was completely exhausted. It was really difficult to drive to school, which looking back is terrible and scary.

It was rough that I kept just staying up so that I would be running off of adrenaline. Not a good time. It made everything worse.

Austin

A pretty negative coping habit I have is feeling sorry for myself. I didn't realize how much I did at the beginning of high school. It didn't help.

There's a difference between just letting myself feel and feeling sorry for myself. I did a lot of crying. It's okay to cry. You know, a lot of men feel this obligation to be "masculine" and not cry. But it's okay to cry because if you bottle it up, you're just going to one day burst. It's not going to be pretty when you do, so it's okay to cry.

When I say feeling sorry for myself, I mean it differently than letting myself cry or whatever. It's like this: I think it's okay for me to have a day. A day to sit, to cry, to fall to pieces, and to feel bad for myself, but after that, I need to get up. I guess it sounds a little harsh, but I have to tell myself, *Get up, you can cope while you live.* There's a way to do it.

I have to find a happy medium because if I sit in my sorrows having a pity party, they're going to swallow me. Nobody deserves that. Nobody should go through that, and I shouldn't put myself through that.

WHAT ARE STRESSORS?

A stressor is any event, environment, change, condition, fear, or pressure that places strain on you—ranging on a scale from everyday inconveniences like losing your keys to major emergencies like being in a car wreck. Smaller stressors may have brief effects, such as experiencing passing feelings of frustration. Major life situations can have extended and even traumatic effects draining your coping abilities; with these big stressors, even small things can start to build up and leave you unable to cope. If you don't have what you need to deal with your stress, you become overloaded.

Everyone has a different set of stressors, and any situation that feels difficult, painful, frightening, or beyond your control can be a stressor. While some are utterly unbothered by performing in front of a crowd and are even energized by it, others find it a source of terror. Some people thrive in academic environments, while others find them crushingly stressful. Common stressors for teenagers include:

* Academic expectations, responsibilities, and frustrations

* Personal expectations, responsibilities, and frustrations

* Social difficulties with friends, peers, and significant others

* Family and parental problems—conflicts, divorce, financial difficulties

* Troubled or dangerous home, neighborhood, or school environment

* Moving homes or schools

* Health problems—self or loved ones

* Death of a loved one

Knowing your stressors can help you keep your finger on your mental and physical pulse. Also, awareness of your stressors means when one is upcoming in your life (like a big test or applying for college), you can begin to cope in advance. Even if you aren't familiar with your stressors right now, you can start to pay attention to your stress responses to identify situations that make you uncomfortable or unhappy. Everyone has some stressors they may not notice or discover there are once-comfortable relationships in their lives that have shifted.

Like the mood trackers mentioned in previous chapters, it can be helpful to track your current stressors. There are stressor trackers available on the author's website for free download.

This sample stressor tracker shows how filling it out can help reveal patterns in your activities, interactions, and emotions. Because depression can affect memory and functioning, it can be hard to see how your stressors impact you, but trackers can help document this over time. Download a free blank version for you to use on the author's website at christiecognevich.com. *Illustration by Christie Cognevich*

Stressor trackers like this one can help determine potential triggers and patterns in your activities, interactions, and emotions. Download a free blank version for you to use on the author's website at christiecognevich.com. *Illustration by Christie Cognevich*

DATE: 5/2

STRESSFUL EVENT	THOUGHTS & RESPONSES	COPING STRATEGY
Late (again) because I had to make breakfast and get Sean and Ava to school first. Detention for tardies on Saturday.	If I could trust that Mom would get the little ones up and ready for school, I wouldn't be late all the time. I'm angry at everyone, but especially her.	I went into the bathroom, closed my eyes, and counted to ten over and over until I could breathe. I spent lunch in the library to avoid Mrs. Clark or else I'd probably get another detention.

Stressor trackers like this one can help determine potential triggers and patterns in your activities, interactions, and emotions. Download a free blank version for you to use on the author's website at christiecognevich.com. *Illustration by Christie Cognevich*

FEELING STRESSED

Stress can be helpful. When you feel stressed, your body prepares itself automatically to act in the face of danger (thanks, body!). However, your body doesn't know how to distinguish whether that danger is a herd of elephants stampeding straight for you or a standardized test or abstract fears and anxieties about your future. In all of these instances, your body responds similarly: many hormones increase to signal your body to get ready for pushing oxygen-rich blood as quickly as possible to your muscles and brain to aid in thinking, fighting, and running. You probably know these physical sensations already:

- Your breathing gets faster to get more oxygen into your bloodstream.

- Your heartbeat speeds up, and blood pressure rises to push blood along quicker.

- Any body parts or processes not essential to immediate survival get less blood and energy—for example, your toes and fingers might feel cold or tingly because of decreased blood flow.

- Digestion is only needed for long-term survival, so your body's shifting priorities away from digestion to fuel the brain and muscles is often experienced as a nervous, fluttery feeling in the stomach. That's your digestion slowing down as your energy is redirected elsewhere.

- You might notice that you feel tense—this is because your muscles are getting ready to act, just like a cat tensing in preparation to spring on its unsuspecting toy.

There's nothing wrong with these sensations in general! Stress helps you do what you need to do in a difficult moment. You can sometimes even enjoy your body's natural stress responses—for example, many people enjoy visiting Halloween haunted houses and riding roller coasters. In this case, you have some measure of control over exiting the experience, and then your stress response (theoretically) goes away after you are no longer there.

There are other physical stress responses, but these are some of the most common. If you feel these physical sensations—even if you aren't fully conscious of what you're stressed about—you are responding to a stressor in some way. Take a moment to acknowledge your feelings and identify what stressors are producing that feeling.

Where do you feel stress in your body?

Chloe

When I'm stressed, I know because I generally feel very nauseous. I want to move my hands a lot. Not like they start shaking, but I get this urge to move them around. I was studying for finals last year, and my body just felt too antsy. I wanted to get up and jump around. I also felt so nauseous that I wanted to cry. I just took deep breaths (using 4-7-8 breathing) until it started to fade and took a break from studying. The 4-7-8 breathing pattern is when you breathe in through your nose for four seconds, pause and hold your breath for seven seconds, then push your breath out through your mouth for eight seconds.

Alyssa

My stomach and my neck feel like they're frozen. My heart, which is usually slow from a medical condition, starts to beat faster, and I feel sweaty. Sometimes my heart slows down, and I feel like the world is coming down around me. Then I have to fight off my body's urge to shut down on me. It makes my head hurt badly because I'm fighting for feeling in my legs, arms, et cetera, and my body is not responding.

I don't always know how stressed I am at the moment. At the beginning of almost every night last year, I was unable to sleep because I kept crying and freaking out. I just thought I was dumb and worrying too much. Later my psychiatrist told me that I was experiencing panic attacks because my body became immune to my antidepressant medication. Sometimes your body can build up a tolerance to antidepressants, and they stop working.

One time that happened when I had a panic attack in school, and I just felt like there was a hole in my stomach, so I started mentally panicking.

Then my body started to react worse, so I had to lie on the ground and slowly take in deep breaths. I was forced to do this for a long time because every time I would stop, I would get that nervous feeling in my stomach again. Eventually, I was able to relax my body, and then after my body relaxed, I was able to tell myself that everything was going to be okay.

Grace

I feel stress in my neck first and anxiety in my stomach. I find acknowledging my anxiety is powerful in controlling it, even if all I say is, "I feel anxious right now."

Emma

I didn't know I felt stress in my forehead, jaw, neck, and shoulders until I did a group counseling "body scan" activity where everyone had to clench and then relax each part of our bodies from the top of our heads down to our toes. At first, it was funny trying to figure out how to clench the top of my head, but then as we worked our way down tensing up and releasing, I realized there were a lot of places already tensed up. The conscious effort of paying attention to my body to clench my muscles taught me where I was holding a lot of tension without realizing it. Some people can do the activity alone without someone walking them through, but I like having a voice to follow and focus on because my attention drifts sometimes. There are lots of mindfulness body scan videos on YouTube that walk you through.

Stress ruins my sleep, too. I have a reoccurring dream about being in school that I get when I'm stressed out, even if it's not school that's bothering me. I dream that I'm in a school building looking all over for a classroom that I can't find, I'm running late, and if I don't get there, I can't take an important test to pass the class. It's usually a math class, which I've always felt is my worst subject.

The building looks different every time I dream it, but it's always a huge maze-looking school with all kinds of stairways and elevators all over the place. Everything has that cold nightmare feeling to it.

I can't find the right classroom because I've been skipping class for weeks. I already feel terrified that I'm going to miss the test—and I have no idea what's going to be on the test—but I'm also filled with shame and dread because the teacher and everyone in the classroom will know I've been skipping. It's just this whole emotional ball of fear and shame.

I don't think I've ever found the right room in my dream. Then I wake up miserable and exhausted.

THE PROBLEM WITH LONG-TERM STRESS

You are under stress when your body's responses prepare you for a physical action to deal with a short-term issue. When humans were cavemen, you needed to be able to run from dangerous animals or avoid eating spoiled meat. If you see a situation that looks dangerous—like a herd of elephants about to stampede—your emotional response of fear helps you avoid it and stay safe. If you see food that has gone bad, your emotional response of disgust prevents you from eating it—a way in which your body naturally prevents you from eating poisonous or dangerous foods.

That's why there are no "good" or "bad" emotions; even emotions we might categorize as "bad" have their benefits. If there *is* a stampede of elephants coming right for you, your natural biological response means your body is now prepared to run or fling yourself out of the way. Once you've acted, your body gradually returns to normal, and you feel better. Fear and discomfort can be beneficial to help you hide or avoid a dangerous person in a single moment. Stress can even help push you to develop new skills in a moment—when you're at the edge of your knowledge and comfort zone, stress can push you to make the most of it and grow. Few people would ever learn to successfully drive if stress didn't equip us to make spur-of-the-moment physical and mental decisions in a pinch.

You can deal with some stress. Too much stress that can't be acted upon, worked off, or put to use, however, becomes a problem—for example, if you're very stressed, but there is no immediate moment of life-or-death danger. Our bodies are pretty limited in how they deal with the drawn-out emotional stress caused by modern issues. Preparing to run physically won't help you respond to someone's comment online, especially since the long-term emotional fallout of that might stretch over days or weeks. If you need to take an important test, your rapid heartbeat, accelerated breathing, and nervous stomach will probably not feel helpful. Even though the test may seem life or death to you emotionally, our stress responses evolved out of physical survival concerns, not the modern concerns we have today. (Yes, your body is obsolete technology! It's doing the best it can, but it's a calculator living in a smartphone world.)

And what if you do feel endangered not in a single moment like an elephant stampede, but over the long term—like an unstable, abusive living condition or a state of worry about potential violence at school? If you're in a state of heightened stress about your safety over a long time, it's exhausting and impossible for your body to maintain this constant awareness. Emotionally, this state isn't designed for happiness, and physically, it isn't designed for the long term.

Human bodies are fascinating and powerful survival machines when placed under physical stress, but when you perpetually struggle to survive, it means you never feel safe or stable enough to *thrive*. Getting stuck in survival mode means being in a state of crisis preventing you from healthy patterns—your thoughts start spiraling repetitively, your heartbeat starts racing or stuttering, your sleep becomes interrupted, your physical resources are depleted so that your immune system is weak. When in this state, all you can do is react to what is happening to you physically, mentally, and emotionally, but you might feel like you can't ever get *beyond* that to making active choices instead of reactive ones. It feels like you're no longer in control, and that's psychologically terrifying.

To be clear, the biological response itself isn't bad—as you can tell, it exists for a reason. Its purpose is to keep your body in a state of awareness and tension for when it needs to act to save you in a life-or-death situation. Once you get past the immediate moment of life or death, lingering in survival mode prevents growth and can start to harm you. Either your brain can work to protect you, or it can learn and grow, but not both at the same time.

What kinds of situations are stressful for you?

Blake

Testing! I can't even begin to describe how many times I've been in a stressful moment when it felt like my body decided to betray me completely.

Once when I was taking a big standardized test, I felt my stomach start to cramp up, I started sweating, and I knew then it was going to be a terrible day.

I know this is maybe gross, but it's the truth, and I think (I hope) a lot of people will see what I'm talking about. I was trying so hard to take the stupid test, but I kept having to ask permission to go to the bathroom. I was sitting on the toilet, looking at my chances of a bright future down the toilet, I guess! It was not fun. Bye, life! Bye, future career!

Cailyn

My parents are big yellers, and it stresses me out so much. I freak out when I hear them start yelling. I lock the door and think, *Don't come in here; don't come in here.*

I don't like it when people angry yell. Angry yelling—instant tears. I get shivers down my back. The whole thing with my parents makes me more anxious about everything and paranoid. I always have a constant fear of what I'm doing wrong.

They say my name and I'm scared of what I've done.

Alyssa

I have a medical condition that makes me pass out sometimes. It often makes me feel that I cause too many problems for other people. It's stressful always to worry that I'm going to ruin something or be too much trouble.

Sometimes if I'm off with my friends, I'm forced to return home because I need to take my medicine. For example, when I go out, my parents tell all of my friends that they need to be on the lookout for me at all times because I could pass out. My friends are understanding, but then again, I feel that I'm more of a problem to bring along places.

And I feel like I've ruined plans or events if I have an episode. There will be situations where I feel like I am about to pass out, but I will not tell anyone because I want to handle it on my own.

I did this at my boyfriend's surprise party. Everyone was having fun in the pool and playing around, but I was struggling to stay conscious. I knew that if I said that I wasn't feeling well, my boyfriend would stop anything he was doing to take care of me and make sure that I was all right again. I thought that it would ruin the party, and I didn't want everyone's attention.

Ah, yes, *attention*, that's another joke that people love to tell me that bothers me. Whenever I would wake up from being unconscious during an event with a lot of adults, there would always be someone to make some joke about me just wanting "all of the attention" on me.

I wake up on the floor with a crowd of people surrounding me, so I'm already uncomfortable. I don't need people teasing me too. I don't understand why that is such a common joke to be told while I'm just regaining feeling in my body! I know they are just trying to make light of the situation because everyone gets uncomfortable, but it always makes me feel so self-conscious and more stressed out.

Alyssa passes out due to her health issues and is often teased that she is just doing it for the attention, which stresses her even more. *Illustration by Kate Haberer*

CHAPTER SIX

EFFECTIVELY DEALING
WITH STRESS

If you are often overstressed, this will bleed over into your thought patterns, social relationships, and more. If you've ever accidentally snapped at someone over something small or slammed a door after having a bad day, you're draining off some of that physical stress response that gets you wound up and ready for action. Or you might feel antsy and unable to concentrate when you've got that excess adrenaline buzzing through your body, so you go out and do something to blow off steam. When your brain and body rarely level out to get the healthy rest they need, you will inevitably turn to coping strategies to help bring yourself relief.

Many of the healthy ways to cope physically are things you've heard before: get enough sleep, drink enough water, eat healthily, stay physically active. These habits work because they return your body to equilibrium, the state of balance before your body's physical defenses activated. Exercising, hydrating, and healthily feeding yourself will work off your adrenaline and muscular tension, as well as restore much-needed nutrients to your depleted body, which spent those nutrients fueling your stress response.

But when your body has geared up for action, sometimes the actions you take can be impulsive, with short-term benefits that don't outweigh the long-term consequences. Ineffective coping habits, including drugs, alcohol, and unsafe sex, can fuel negative self-talk, self-harm, and depression.

Effective coping habits vary from person to person, but the goal is to satisfy your body's need to do something in a distressing time without having regrets later. Some of these require a lot of time and practice but can be quite effective in changing your mental patterns and behavioral habits for the better.

- Involve yourself in sports and other physical outlets.

- Involve yourself in the arts and other creative outlets.

- Intentionally engage with stressful situations under safe circumstances—for example, if public speaking stresses you, join the speech team, or if an important scholarship or job interview is upcoming, practice with a teacher or counselor beforehand.

- Allow yourself to stop short of perfection. Acknowledge sometimes that the best work is finished work. It doesn't always have to be gold plated.

- Notice your mind's clearest, most productive times. Are you a morning person or a night person? When do you feel you have the most energy to get things done? Try to arrange your tasks so that the more important ones get done during your more focused, energetic times to make them feel easier.

- Practice long-term time management techniques by looking ahead at what tasks are upcoming. Keep a planner or calendar and build the habit of checking it.

- Practice short-term time management and giving yourself breaks. If you have a hard time concentrating for long stretches or are easily distracted by too many tabs open on your browser (aren't we all?), there are timers to help you break down bigger tasks into smaller bite-sized pieces. Check out tomato-timer.com; it's a set of timers for work (twenty-five minutes), short breaks (five minutes), and long breaks (ten minutes). For every work timer, you get a short break timer in between. For every four work timers, you get a long break. If these timings don't work for you, you can also customize them.

- Learn some relaxation and breathing exercises. You don't have to start on your own—there are apps like Calm and Insight Timer, which have lots of free content in addition to paid content where you can follow along on the exercises. Building small skills like noticing your breathing, your thoughts, and your tension levels can help give you better control over your mind and body during challenging times.

- Check out some useful apps to guide you to ride through stressful moments: Calm Harm, Clear Fear, and Woebot are a few. Remember, they aren't a substitute for crisis help if you need it, but they can get you through difficulties and build your coping skills when you aren't in immediate crisis.

- Work on your self-talk and challenge your negative self-perceptions lovingly. Your thoughts may not always be positive, but they can be neutral or accepting. For example, *I'm fat and unattractive and suck at sports* is a hopeless and harmful way of talking to yourself. You may not feel ready to tell yourself, *I may not always feel unattractive when I find people love me for more than my body.* You may not feel like telling yourself, *I feel this way at the moment, but my body isn't stuck in a permanent shape.* But start by telling yourself, *I wouldn't mind feeling healthier.* Build your thoughts up from there.

- Surround yourself with a positive support system and encouraging people, whether in person or online. You may not find everything you need from one particular friend or friend group; you might find it's easier to talk about some subjects with different people.

- Take a break from stressful situations. Your mind needs breaks too. Play a video game, listen to music, talk to your friends, pet your animals, look at the internet, read a book, whatever helps you unplug. The key is to not overdo the breaks into marathon distraction sessions. Harder said than done—it requires practice.

How do you cope with your stress?

Austin

I cope by being a performer. By performing, by rehearsing, by saying, *Okay, I have this show to do, and I have this audience to entertain, and it's time to put on the face.* Or the character, depending on what I'm doing—whether it's a concert, comedy show, or stage show. Even little short films that I've done. It's time to put on the mask and time to become the character. That's my positive coping. It took me a long time to learn how to do that.

There are two ways of going about that. I can say, *Well, I've coped because I've performed.* But then you can also easily say that I'm holding it all inside because I'm putting on these faces. But there's a healthy way of doing it. It's about finding a happy medium. I can do that by *admitting* so-and-so hurt me because of what they did to me, but I'm going to let it go. I'm not pretending like it didn't happen while I'm acting.

Then I go into a happy place, being in front of an audience and entertaining them and telling them jokes. Through the happiness that they're bringing me, I can let go of the sadness. I have to acknowledge it so I can let it go through performance.

I don't talk about my problems that much at all in public, or at least, the deep ones. There are a lot of people that post about it on their social media. I'm not comfortable with that because I'm a private person. Since I don't do that, I relate my problems to an audience when I'm performing in front of them. I turn what I'm experiencing into a joke. I need to find the funny in my life. That's a lesson I've learned, and it's something that I continue to believe in. You have to find the funny and laugh.

I think the healthy way to do it is if you don't have a creative outlet for yourself and if you can't find a creative outlet, then talk to somebody. Get a therapist. So many people are thrown off when they believe that a therapist is there to tell you what to do, but they're not. They're there to listen to you and understand you and help you. There's a difference.

Find outlets. Find friends that support you. If you're in a friend group that doesn't support you, find a new one because you may be alone for a minute, but that's okay. It's okay to be alone because that gives you time to look at you. It's always okay to be alone, and it's okay also to remember that you're not always going to be alone.

Then when you get out there and talk to somebody, you'll be surprised. People want to listen, people do, and they will.

Grace

When I went through depression as a result of my mother's addiction and subsequent death, journaling was a really powerful tool for coping for me. It helped me to say things that I felt I couldn't say or wasn't allowed to feel. Reading was also a numbing activity for me. In hindsight, I'm not sure it was completely healthy, but it was my escape.

Emma

When I stress about someone or something that happened, I like to write letters I'll never send. I pour it all out—all the hurt, all the nasty things I want to say. The key is to make sure you type it somewhere that isn't easy to send, like in your notes. Don't forget that. That way, after you write it all out, you don't accidentally hit send, or the impulse of the send button being right there doesn't tempt you. The point isn't to send the letters because definitely I've probably written a lot of things that shouldn't be said and I don't even mean.

The point is feeling like I've poured it out or maybe even get the satisfaction of saying something mean without actually doing it. It helps me blow off steam and get rid of some negative impulses without hurting anyone. Fake letters are great, *and* you can put all the clever comebacks you thought of five minutes too late in them.

To cope with her stress, Emma writes letters she will never send and watches cooking shows so she can imagine herself eating the food without actually overeating. *Illustration by Kate Haberer*

Make sure you delete any that you don't want around for people to find later.

I'm not going to lie; I do the same thing with shopping. I fake shop to make myself feel better, but I don't have to worry about spending money I can't afford or being wasteful. I'll click on things I want in Amazon and fill up my cart, then delete them. I mentally get the satisfaction of buying things for myself because I clicked the button.

Be careful not to have any automatic purchases turned on. I do it in real life, too. I push things around in the cart to get the satisfaction of having them, then bring them back to where they belong. Don't abandon a cart full of stuff that people have to put back; put your stuff back yourself. Psychologically, I feel like I put the thing in the cart and pushed it around a bit, and that satisfies me.

Lastly, comfort eating is a problem for me. I struggle with being one of those people who eat their feelings. I like to cook and experiment in the kitchen, so whenever I get the urge to eat, I'll turn on cooking and baking shows. That may not work for everyone—it might make them want to eat more—but for me, it gives me the feeling of looking at all the foods and drinking them imaginatively without having to eat them. It's window-shopping for eating. I like the food competitions with kids because they'll stop and help each other finish or share ingredients. I find that refreshing and relaxing.

I didn't realize how many "fake" things I do to get the feeling of having done them without negative consequences, but these things do help me cope with my feelings.

Also, find what gives you any joy no matter what's going on. For me, that's my cat. I have a friend who doesn't have any pets, so she will make people FaceTime her with their pets to cheer her up.

My cat always makes me laugh. When I do my homework, my cat likes to try to play with and bite my pens and highlighters. He has a white stripe on his face, and I accidentally colored it with highlighter when he kept messing with it while I was using it. He looked stupid and wonderful. I look for the little joy in the ridiculous things he does.

One time, I was upset so my friend came over. I was crying, so she hugged me, and my cat bit her. My cat never bites anyone; he's a cuddly lap cat. He normally loves her and will absolutely ignore me for her to pet and scratch him behind the ears. He thought I was crying because she was hurting me, and then both of us couldn't help but laugh because it was adorable that he thought he was defending me. Even on my worst days, I know my cat loves me.

That helps me deal with things, knowing something small and fuzzy and sweet exists in the world like that.

Blake

I unplug with music. Happy music, sad music, angry music, whatever—it doesn't matter. I put my headphones on and dive into the sound. It helps me with my anxiety to focus on the lyrics or the music instead of my thoughts sometimes.

In the next chapter, we'll explore some more strategies for and anecdotes about maintaining your mental health through serious life issues like family dysfunction, academic expectations, social media use, interpersonal relationships, body image, and choosing your future path.

CHAPTER SEVEN

THE STRESSORS

BODY IMAGE, HEALTH ISSUES,
SEXUALITY AND GENDER,
ACADEMICS, AND SOCIAL MEDIA

When we explore various life stressors, addressing or avoiding the stressor may not completely fix your depressed feelings except in rare cases. As I mentioned in an earlier chapter, depression doesn't necessarily need a cause or a trigger. (And it is, unfortunately, true that even "solved" problems sometimes leave bruises that take a little longer to fade.) Stressors and the physical stress responses they provoke can leave you continually feeling in battle with life itself, arrows raining down from all directions. Recognizing your areas of emotional strain and how your body and mind respond to them can help you face them in better armor built out of clearer understanding, control, and purpose.

Seven in ten American teenagers report depression as a significant problem in their community among people their age, and school pressures regularly top the list of teenage stressors. Eighty-eight percent of teenagers report they feel pressure to get good grades, and among those, over 60 percent report feeling *a lot* of pressure around their grades. At the same time, 70 percent of these teenagers wish they had more good friends, and a quarter of them feel like they come across people who try to put them down almost every single day.[1]

Meanwhile, social media remains a conflicted source of and help for stress. The American Psychological Association notes, "For more than half of [teenagers] (55 percent), [social media] provides a feeling of support. The flipside, however, is that nearly half say social media makes them feel judged (45 percent), and nearly two in five (38 percent) report feeling bad about themselves as a result of social media use."[2]

Anything can be a stressor if it bothers you. Of course, this means it's impossible to cover all the stressors in your life, so this book will stick to some common, broad categories. The point of these stories is not necessarily to show the "perfect" way to deal—life is messy, and these real-life stories aren't lectures on exactly how to do things right. They're honest reflections of the tangled messiness of life.

Many of these anecdotes address how these individuals recognize they responded in a way that made their problems worse. Many of these anecdotes address how they wish they would have responded. In some cases, there is a positive resolution, and in some cases, the problem is ongoing.

Let's hear from some people about the stressors they've experienced in life.

BODY IMAGE

How has your body image impacted you and your stress?

Austin

I think the best way to describe my body image problem is I have a problem with telling myself that I'm not good enough. I'm not physically attractive enough as I am.

There's not a time I can remember not thinking that I wasn't ugly or fat. I always had cousins that were more active than me. I had siblings that were more attractive than me. You know, the cousins were more active, they were skinnier. Siblings were prettier.

For a long time, I didn't know who I was because of my body image. I was like, *Well, who is this blob?* There's not one time I looked at myself in the mirror and said, "Perfect." Some people will choose to look in the mirror and find imperfections and flaws, and

I do that. Some people choose to look in the mirror and say, "This is what I got, and this is what I want to live with." And then some people will choose and look in the mirror and say, "I look great!" And, well, I will always say, "I look great . . . for *me*."

I think my body issues come from family and friends saying good things about everybody else but not complimenting me. It was both a lack of positive comments and a lot of little negative comments.

You know, such things as, "You're going to eat *that*? Oh, you're going to blow up!"

What I did that was *not* healthy was that for many years I kept it bottled up inside. And for many years, it contributed to many problems that I now have—I have an eating disorder.

I don't like to talk about that, but now it's hard for me sometimes because of my body image. It's hard for me to eat right.

Sometimes I go one week with eating only one meal a day or two weeks of only eating one meal a day. I'll drop ten pounds, and then sometimes I can eat three meals a day and snacks. So it's never a healthy balance, and that's something I have to deal with all the time.

Which, if you haven't eaten for about forty-eight hours, you start to become mean towards others. I knew I had to stop that because I'm not a mean person unless I don't eat, and then I become very upset. In addition to just being physically unhealthy, it was making me not *me*.

As far as unhealthy coping, either I'm stress eating, or I'm just not eating. Any addiction is bad, but a *non*addiction like refusing food and keeping it all bottled up, that's not good either.

When I feel at peace with my body is whenever I'm onstage, whether I'm a character or doing stand-up comedy. It's an out-of-body experience. I can't explain it, but what I can say is that when I get on that stage, and I get in front of that audience, it's my party. It's my show. Let me be the host. And when I'm the host, I'm in my host mode. I can be fabulous.

Accepting my body is like a grieving process—sad, angry, but eventually accepted. Okay, this is my body; this is the machinery.

Now, what are the accessories that I can use to make this thing work? I'm going to have a good personality. I'm going to have a good sense of humor.

I'd rather joke about my imperfections than joke about my perfections. I use my comedy a lot as a coping habit. It's this gesture of, of before you can humiliate me, I am going to get me before you can. I'm going to tell you what's wrong with me, and it's going to be funny because it *is* funny.

I think my jokes, my impressions, my songs, they feel like this beam of light in me. It's what's gotten me through the tough times, and it's taught me, you are enough, you were enough. That's when I feel most at peace with myself is when I'm on a stage or in front of a camera.

Jael

I'm painfully self-conscious about my front teeth. I don't think I had a terrible fixation on my teeth when I was little, although I did find a journal I wrote years back worrying that my two front teeth were going to come in as giant bunny teeth because a girl in my class told me that after your front teeth fell out, you couldn't touch your gums there, or the new teeth would come in huge.

When my new front teeth came in, they looked fine except for the tiniest little thing, just a slight unevenness across the bottom of my front teeth where they had these small ridges. A lot of new teeth have them, but generally, they smooth out after time because they wear down when you chew.

One day, my mom brought me to the dentist for a standard cleaning. While we were in the waiting room, she kept trying to get me to agree to let the dentist file my front teeth down just a little to get rid of the ridges and make them even all the way across. Given that I hate the dentist and even getting them cleaned was stressful, that was a pretty definite *no* from me.

I should have known when she just said, "Okay," and dropped it that something was up. She never says okay and lets anything go if she wants it.

Jael's mother asked the dentist to file the ridges of her teeth, even after Jael said no. *Illustration by Kate Haberer*

As should have been obvious to me, she secretly told the dentist to do it anyway, which I found out—surprise!—when he came in and just started filing them. It happened quickly and then was done, but it was super upsetting. It was kind of not cool to expect the five-second dentist glance after cleaning, and instead, get the gloved hands wielding a file and permanently modifying your smile. There's that whole minor "it's my mouth" boundary issue with my mom.

As the universe's a grand joke, the ridges are still there just a little. My mother isn't allowed to go to the dentist with me anymore.

I remind myself, I'm the only one who notices. No one else cares about the world's tiniest flaw. A year later, my mom didn't even remember she did that and was just like, "Really? I did that? I'm sorry, I think your teeth are fine."

I let someone else's criticism get into my head, and it isn't even a thing.

Leila

I play soccer, and I was never the fastest player in my sport. When I was younger, it messed with me mentally. I used to think it was my weight. I talked down on myself and told myself I'd never be a good enough soccer player or skinny enough to be considered "good at my sport."

My older sister is naturally thin, so I used to always compare my body type to hers. As I got older, I realized that our body types weren't the same, so there was no comparison.

I also felt the same way that very few girls at my school had my body type, so I felt overweight when reality I was very fit. I was often more fit than everyone else from all the sports training I did. Over the summer, I worked with our team's trainer and had abs for the first time in my life, but I was still unhappy.

Sometimes I would skip dinner or breakfast. There were some days when all I would eat was lunch because I wanted to be slimmer.

I found out that for me, eating healthier goes a longer way to keeping me good and playing well than working out every day. If I'm not okay mentally, it will show through my body.

Audrey

Proportionally, my body has been the same my entire life—a fat body to be precise. I wore a women's size sixteen in middle school, and I wasn't even finished growing.

I concluded at a young age, in my heart, if not in my head, I would never be less than fat. If this is what my body wanted to do, it's what it was going to do, and I could spend the rest of my life tormenting myself or making peace with it. Easier said than done, of course.

I remember trying on a dress, noticing a particularly flattering angle. I was thrilled at how "beautiful" I looked, only to turn and look "hideous" from a different angle. At that moment, I realized how meaningless it was to obsess over how my body looked. Even thin people have "unflattering" angles.

My first strategy for living in a fat body, the one I adopted in my early teens, was to say I didn't care. My body didn't matter because I was a smart girl, a brain on a stick, all that mattered was school and career.

Ignoring my feelings, however, defaulted into shame. If I can't think about it, can't talk about it, there must be something wrong with it. And if there's something wrong with it, but I can't think about it, it can never be "fixed," and so how I treat my body ultimately doesn't matter.

I wish instead I could have processed through my feelings about my body because, what I know now—the body is intimately connected with all factors of life, including mental health. I spent so long ignoring my body; I didn't learn how to listen to it very well.

Listening to my body and meeting its needs—for nourishment, rest, pleasure—have greatly improved all facets of my life.

When I'm feeling down about my body, I play what I think of as the gratitude game. I start at my feet and work my way up, thanking each part for its service. Focusing on what my body *does*, rather than how it *looks* or *feels*, brings me from a judgmental mindset based on outside looks to looking at my body's value.

HEALTH ISSUES

How have health issues impacted you and your stress?

Alyssa

My health problems first started on my thirteenth birthday. I was getting ready for my birthday dinner, and I passed out in the shower.

The shower was really hot, so my family thought maybe it was that. Also, I'm a huge wimp, and everyone knows when I see things like blood I pass out, so then we thought maybe since I was on my period, I saw some blood, and it made me pass out.

Then I started passing out every single day all that year, and the next year when I started high school, it went up to twice a day. I was super stressed out because my family kept taking me to all these doctors, and no one knew what was wrong with me. They knew it was something called vasovagal syncope with postural orthostatic hypotension—my blood pressure drops low and I pass out, but no one knew why.

Doctors said I was a medical mystery. I kept having to go to the hospital, get tests done, miss school. Even though they didn't know what was making me faint, I had to go through trial and error with all different kinds of medicine to see if it would help.

When I started at my new high school, we still didn't have any answers. It was literally within the first couple of weeks of starting there that I passed out and broke my tailbone when I fell. Since I was a fall risk, I ended up having to stay out of school for three weeks. During my first three weeks of high school, when everyone was getting to know each other and making new friends, I wasn't there.

When I came back, all of my old friends were acting super weird and distant. At lunch, we used to sit together, but now I was on the outside fringes. Then they stopped inviting me to things because they didn't want to deal with me passing out.

My mom and my best friend's mom had been friends forever and had never fought before. But then when everyone started leaving me out, they got in a huge fight over it.

There I was at a new school missing way too much class with a mystery health problem, and now I had no friends. I felt like I was stressing the teachers out also with them having to help me catch up and having to worry that I might pass out in their class. I felt like a burden on my friends and family and everyone.

Since I didn't fit in with my old friends, and they kicked me out of their friend group, I started eating lunch in the bathroom. On one of the days I was absent, I found later there was an announcement about no eating in the bathrooms, but I missed it, which was kind of funny.

We still don't have a full answer about my medical problems, but it turns out that any extreme state makes my heart rate too slow and blood pressure drop. If I'm too hot, too cold, too excited, too sad, I pass out. Since I've passed out so much, I have memory problems now, too. The goal for my doctors is to make sure my medication keeps me physically in a sort of calm middle state.

I have to take several different medicines all throughout the day. Some of my pills speed up my heart rate while my other pills calm me down. I experience strange side effects like hallucinations, full-body goose bumps, nausea, dizziness, and many more strange occurrences out of my control.

Some days my medicine makes it so that I can't stop talking. No matter what I'm thinking of, it will come out of my mouth.

Other days I will believe that I am holding a full conversation with people when in reality, I'm just blankly staring at them, imagining that I'm responding to what they are saying.

I am embarrassed because I feel that I'm not in full control of my body or my words. I get very stressed and sad if I think about this too much.

In the end, making better friends helped me cope. It's kind of like the best revenge when you're getting kicked while you're down is getting up and living well anyway.

Charlie

For the longest time, I knew my career path. I was going to be a
zoologist and study animals out in the field. I studied animals in
depth for years. I even got a volunteer job at the zoo where I worked
for almost four years, and I job-shadowed the zoo's veterinarian.

Something strange happened between the ages of fifteen and
seventeen, though. I developed a skin condition called photosensi-
tivity, so I couldn't be in direct sunlight without experiencing pain
and burning. I couldn't tan, and I couldn't just stick it out.

I had to reevaluate everything. If I couldn't be in the sun, I
couldn't study out in the field. It was a huge blow to learn that
things can be taken away from you because of nothing you did to
earn that loss.

SEXUALITY AND GENDER

**How have your sexuality and identity impacted you and your
stress?**

Audrey

When I was in sixth grade, the boys and girls got sent into sep-
arate rooms to watch videos about "our changing bodies." In
seeing the details about puberty—especially how girls would get
"boy crazy"—I thought, *Bring it on!* It looked exciting.

By eighth grade, I started seeing the effects of puberty on
my classmates, but not myself. Or rather, I was physically going
through puberty with acne and a growing chest, but the "boy cra-
ziness" part hadn't set in, and that seemed like the most important
part! I was a late bloomer, I figured.

By the time I was sixteen, nothing had changed, except a
growing confusion and despair. My closest friends were boys, but
somehow, I wasn't "girlfriend material."

My male friends were more emotionally intimate with me
than their girlfriends, so I couldn't figure out what was wrong with

me. There was some hidden component of boyfriend/girlfriend relationships I couldn't figure out. I didn't particularly want to.

I was completely satisfied with the relationships I did have, except the social messages distributed everywhere that romantic relationships are the most important relationships.

My self-worth was tied to my (in)ability to form a romantic relationship. *But I'm only sixteen*, I thought. *I'm just a late bloomer.*

I gave up. I figured out that the hidden component was the sexual attraction, and I didn't feel it. I'd never heard anyone talk about *not* having sexual feelings—all the talk at school and church was about resisting temptation.

I was the only one who had ever existed who didn't feel that. Who could I talk to? Who would understand? If I found someone, what would I say?

I didn't have the vocabulary to make sense of what I felt. I was born broken; I would always be alone, isolated.

That answer didn't satisfy me, though; how could it? I spent years trying to figure out what was going on. I came to believe I couldn't possibly be the only one.

Finally, I did an internet search for "asexual" and found the Asexual Visibility and Education Network. There it was! An entire community of people all over the world who also didn't experience sexual attraction!

I wish I could say that I solved my problem. It took months for me to accept my asexuality and years to be confident with it. But finding others like me was a start, and one of the defining moments of my life.

I had an insistent friend who wanted me to become like her. I didn't know at the time I was asexual, but I did know I had no interest in sex or dating.

That was unacceptable to her; she even suggested I "practice kissing" on our gay friends to improve my confidence. If I say I don't want to kiss people, that should be the end of the conversation. Also, our gay friends are people and not kissing practice.

Austin

I think the first time I started to think about my sexual orientation was my first sexual encounter. I was thirteen, and it was at—how Southern—a Super Bowl party. A guy about a year or two older than me came up and proceeded to come onto me, and so one thing led to another. He was a lot more experienced than I was. That was probably the first time that I had thought about being gay.

Which in a way, I don't know whether I regret it, but it's interesting because I think a lot of other people would regret it that they didn't have time to think about their sexuality, whereas I felt I was just pushed into knowing what mine was. You know some people, they experiment, and I never got to do that. It was just full-fledged, *Okay, I'm gay.*

I questioned it just for a minute. Being thirteen at the time, I said to myself, *Oh, maybe it's just a phase.* I think deep down, I was sure.

One of my first phrases was "Martini shaken or stirred?" I had a play kitchen as a child, and I'd fix martinis! There was always a little something about me that was out there. When I was little, someone said to my mother, "If you buy him a kitchen set, it's going to turn him gay," like someone comes in with a rainbow-colored cape and zaps me with a wand.

I have two gay uncles that live in another state, and they're fabulous. They have a lot of friends, so that was big for me: some people live their lives, and they're not treated as aliens. There are love and acceptance in the world.

I have one grandmother that's Mother Teresa. She goes to church every Sunday and is a good little Southern woman. At one time, she had high hopes of me becoming a priest. Not anymore.

My other grandmother is this cool old lady, so she's very accepting and very loving. I was visiting her, and we were in her basement doing something, and she said to me, "You know, it's okay to be whoever you want to be."

I didn't have to say anything else. I knew that she knew, and that was comforting.

I don't think I still struggle accepting my sexuality, but growing up in a small town, having other people look at you funny, and having other people know that you're gay, whispering behind your back makes you feel like you have nobody but yourself. That stays with you.

It was hurtful when my father told me recently that he had to "*deal* with me" and had to deal with "eccentric people" like me. I thought, *Why not be eccentric?*

My dad is a guide fisherman, which means he takes tourists fishing. My grandfather was the first guy in the South who did it. They were naturally expecting a fisherman to come out, and a tap dancer did. They had very different expectations of what kind of man I was going to be.

I grew up in a town where if a boy wasn't a fisherman or a hunter or a sportsman, he was considered out there. It was one thing for a girl to be into the theater, but to be a boy? Oh, no. Then to be a boy who does theater and who loves Dolly Parton and Judy Garland and Debbie Reynolds?

My father and I have had a very tumultuous relationship. He's a very quiet person, and I'm not. I wear a lot of makeup because I think you should do what you want to do. If you feel good and you're happy, and you're healthy, then do it. I wear a lot of makeup. It makes me feel good.

My dad was dating this woman who was not particularly fond of me. I don't know why, because I was nice to her, but she didn't like me. Last year she invited me to her family's Christmas gathering, and my father called me and asked me as a Christmas gift if I would not wear makeup to the party. If I could "tone it down" was the words he used.

I tried to be very gracious, but I told him no. I didn't go. I wasn't about to give him the satisfaction of letting him see that it affected me. It did, but I have to tell myself that there's nothing wrong with who I am.

Austin's father asked him to not wear makeup to a Christmas gathering, so Austin decided not to go and instead stay true to himself. *Illustration by Kate Haberer*

I believe that if you are healthy, happy, and loving others and not hurting others, then you should be able to be who you want to, unapologetically.

For anybody who says differently, whether they're a parent, family, whoever, there's no need for that. It's one thing for them to call it out if you're doing something wrong or hurting someone, but I wasn't doing anything wrong. I have to remember anytime I'm feeling judged by someone, a lot of the time it has nothing to do with me, and it's their loss.

Ava

Last year at my school's winter formal dance, I wore a pantsuit with a blazer instead of a dress.

I felt good about myself, until a random guy walked up, looked at me, and said, "You look like a dyke." I didn't even know him.

I was so shocked; I just played it off like I didn't care. "Oh, yeah? Whatever" was my response. I don't know that I even realized until then that people *still* use that word.

ACADEMICS

How have academic pressures impacted you and your stress?

Charlie

I skipped a grade and moved from fifth to seventh grade. Going from a small elementary school, where I was known as the smartest kid, to an honors classroom was a humbling experience. I had taken a lot of pride in feeling special. I wasn't special anymore, so I turned inward. I allowed myself to fade into obscurity.

I went from being a straight-A gifted student in elementary school to As and Bs (with an isolated C) in high school. My entire self-view had been shattered, so I felt like a massive failure on top of my obliterated social life since I'd lost all my friends skipping a grade.

I eventually threw away my mental self-image of me being a "smart" kid. I just wanted to get out of school as quickly as possible.

I wish I had understood that being "the best" is meaningless in such a big world of amazing people.

Audrey

At my high school, we got two points added to our final grade in each course if we had perfect attendance. I felt like I needed those two points to "pass" (which I defined as nothing lower than an A). It was one more area in my life where the bar was set at perfection.

If I didn't have perfect attendance, I wouldn't get those two points, and I would be a slacker, lazy, not worth anything.

One fall, my grandfather received two free airplane tickets to anywhere in the world, and he chose to take me to London.

I agreed . . . on the condition that I wouldn't miss *any* school.

He took me over Thanksgiving break, and we had a wonderful time, but we spent almost as much time in transit as we did in the city because we had to fly in and out so quickly.

Looking back now, I think, (1) *Wow, that was a super rude response to someone who was being incredibly generous to me*, and (2) *Why did I choose school over a week in London?!*

What I know now is that I was making a long-term decision based on a short-term horizon. London is the most dramatic example of some poor choices I made, but I sacrificed a lot of my time and health on the altar of meeting unrealistic—and unnecessary—academic expectations.

I didn't understand that high school, while important, is just one small part of a (statistically) long life. Any "failures" from those years would be temporary setbacks at most, and that who I was or what I did in high school would not define me forever.

Ava

It makes me feel so stupid when you're in class, and you get something back, then everyone's all, "Oh, what did you get?" Then you're forced to share, and then everyone says, "Ohhhh. Oh, no."

The honors students can be awful sometimes. They'll be like, "Oh, you're just in the *regular* classes." So?

Parents and teachers say a lot that grades don't define who you are; it's just a number. But they do matter, or otherwise, they wouldn't care about it.

I wouldn't even listen to any advice I'd give myself for dealing with academic pressures. It's all stuff I've heard before, and I know it is true, and I ignore it anyway.

My "regular" classes don't define me; my not being an honors student doesn't define me. But I do still feel stupid a lot. I deal with it by just crying sometimes.

My parents say, "It's okay if you're trying your hardest!" If my hardest ends up getting a D– grade, then what? Is that okay? They don't act like it's okay, even if I did try.

Like in math, I understand the concepts, and then on the test, I'll make some stupid mistake with the numbers. It isn't that I didn't know how it all worked; I just added wrong or whatever. That's a frustrating thing because it happens all the time.

It can be hard in the moment to remember that I have strong suits: *Oh, I have to keep working at algebra, but I'm good at another class.* That works well in my head until something terrible happens in the class I'm good at, and then I don't feel like I'm good at *anything.* I have to be careful with putting too much pressure on myself to be good at everything and allow myself to make mistakes.

Cailyn

I've been grounded so many times for bad grades, and it just makes the situation so much worse. I'm already upset about my grades.

And even when they're not that bad, where I struggled, and I worked hard to pull out a B–, my parents aren't satisfied with me trying as hard as I can. Now they're acting like this is a disappointment that a B– is the best I can manage and grounding me.

They sometimes act like I want to get bad grades, so they have to punish me to get me to see the "error of my ways." If I'm struggling and I feel like I'm dumb, getting punished on top of that is unhelpful.

Usually, being with my friends helps. They can be a great distraction from falling in a self-loathing hole. Being grounded feels like I can't get out to talk to my friends so I can feel better. Then I have to make the most of seeing them at school until I can get back to them and they remind me of all of my strengths instead of my weaknesses.

Emma

I am a huge people pleaser, which is problematic when it comes to my academics. I'm a good student, but my best grades are in English and history. I'm still good at math and science, but not the best in the class. It's fine. I don't need to be the best in the class in everything.

I'm also not going to force myself to pick a career based in a STEM field just because it's what everyone else thinks is the smart thing to do. Could I probably do it? Sure. Would I be able to go into engineering? Probably, but that's not what I want to major in. This is the first time I've ever put my foot down with the people pleasing and said no, this isn't what I want, and it's not what I'm going to do.

My dad and I have a difficult relationship. He values different things academically. He has no problem making fun of me at dinner every night. I'm going to be living in a cardboard box under a bridge if I think I'm going to become a writer. I'm going to be asking people if they want fries with their order for the rest of my life if I think I'm going to be an artist.

But, as one of my teachers told me, "It takes all kinds to make a world."

Jael

My friend sent me a meme recently about how the voice in your head is awfully bold for something that has literally never accomplished anything . . . ever. I'm making it my background picture on everything.

The voice in my head is pretty critical about a lot of things, but school is where I constantly feel inadequate, but for no real reason.

When I was in second grade, I had a hard time with math. We would do these flash card quizzes, and I couldn't process what I saw on the card fast enough to do the mental math. I remember it well because the sort of desperate, helpless feeling trying to hold a problem in my mind to solve it while I missed two other cards flashing by was just the worst. I would sit there drowning in flash card anxiety, telling myself, *Faster, faster, faster* instead of being able to solve the problem, so I could never catch up.

I hated that class so much. I always loved school and still do, but that class killed math for me early in my life.

Years later, one of my math teachers pointed out that just because I'm not lightning quick doesn't mean I'm bad at it. She was talking about how studies show that the stereotype that girls are bad at math discourages girls and makes them feel like they aren't as good, so their grades get worse in that area.

I had to go look it up, and there's a lot of research that shows girls are discouraged by people, even their teachers, so they think they're bad at it and give up.

That's my big academic stressor now: to accept that I've got the skills. It doesn't have to be the fastest to be done right. I'm not drowning in the flash card anxiety anymore, and I never have to again. When I think of it that way, it's a good feeling. One day, any school struggles are going to be in the past.

SOCIAL MEDIA

How has social media affected you and your stress?

Chloe

My friend—let's call her G—and I used to design binder covers for people at school, so we had a shared Instagram account for our binder art. I was the main one who did the art, but she helped with coloring them sometimes.

One night, I had a different friend sleeping over, and my phone started blowing up with all these weird calls and messages with people asking what was wrong with me. "What's wrong with you? Why would you post that? That's so messed up." I had no idea what was going on.

It turns out that G changed the password to our Instagram account and posted like she was me saying how much "I" hated my mom and how much I wished she would die of cancer.

I was freaking out, and since she changed the password, I couldn't get back into the account to delete the things she'd said as me.

I ended up leaving my other friend upstairs for hours while I went downstairs and talked to my mom about it. My mom called G's dad, and of course, G lied and said she hadn't done anything and blamed me.

Her parents were divorced, so then my mom called G's mom, who was really mad. Her mom drove over to G's dad's house and picked her up and grounded her. G finally ended up confessing then.

I know what she did had a lot to do with her parents getting divorced, which affected her. I also found out later that a few other girls knew ahead of time what G was going to do, and they thought it was funny, so they didn't tell me.

I feel like I ended up just having to be the bigger person in that situation and let it go. It's not that easy because I didn't have control over what went out about me, and everyone just believed it.

G goes to a different school now, but I run into her at things like football games sometimes. The last time I accidentally ran into her, she asked me if I was ever going to unblock her on social media. Wow. *No.*

My mom doesn't control my social media or anything, but she does check now and will make sure I'm not friending people that have made drama in the past. It's good that she helps me keep those boundaries. I don't mind at all.

Now I have different strategies for different social media platforms. You have to have good boundaries with your life. And not share accounts, ha!

For me, I don't feel like Instagram is as intimate. I have a much wider group of people on Instagram, but I don't post as much and nothing too personal. I wish Instagram would take away the "likes" feature entirely. I know everyone was freaking out about them changing it, so you can't see how many likes something has, but I don't mind. I never liked the likes and comments on Instagram. It doesn't feel authentic—I'll post something, and then someone I don't ever talk to will comment with, "Cute!" Why are they commenting? Then I start to wonder and worry—are they being serious or making fun of me? I don't know.

I like using Snapchat for my close friends. I only keep a close group of people on there, and I have no problem whatsoever with blocking someone if I need to. I have a friend who lives in Paris that I met at a camp that we went to and now we work there every summer. Because it's way too expensive to call or text internationally, we talk back and forth via Snap since we only get to see each other in person during the summers.

I like being social, and I will put my phone down and meet new people, but I'm nervous at first. What I'll do is, if it's someone I think I'd like to know, but I'm feeling awkward, I'll ask them for their Snap so that I can message them that way and feel less weird. After we've talked on Snap, I feel much more comfortable speaking in person because now we know each other.

Chloe's friend locked her out of their shared social media account and started posting hateful messages as Chloe. Chloe is now more restrictive with her social media. *Illustration by Kate Haberer*

It's a good way of feeling people out to see who they are, what kind of person they are, just by seeing what and how they post. You can tell a *lot* about people based on that, what they put out there for everyone to see what they think is worth sharing. Or at least, you can tell what sort of things they value by doing that—even if it's not the "real" them that they're posting.

Cailyn

I have a weird relationship with social media. I grew up where the news was saying to everyone, "Social media is terrible! It's going to make you feel terrible about yourself! It's going to make your kids feel terrible about themselves!"

I do notice a difference between my friends' social media and the other accounts I like to follow, like older family members or my parents' friends. They'll go off and post something that they know will be super controversial, and then all the responses are petty. I can't respond to what they post because I get shot down. Anything I say is "stupid" because I'm "too young to understand." I try to avoid all that. It's not worth it.

I think social media is growing up with us, growing up and getting a little better with people my age, teenagers now.

I'm hopeful. I think it can be a force for good, or at least, you have to use it the right way.

Most of the time, I don't get jealous of what I see online because I know deep down that what goes up is just an edited reality, so I follow more art accounts than people. Honestly, I *love* social media in the sense that I follow so many different creative accounts, and it makes me more motivated to do cool, creative stuff. It helped me become my own person creatively.

I think when you use it like that, social media can be very positive. Now, it has become a place of community. For a lot of people like me who have social anxiety and feel isolated, you can find a community of people no matter what kind of person you are. My areas of interest are art and film.

I've found on my end that sometimes being anonymous is good because it can enable you to have a conversation with *anybody*. Just talking to somebody lets you feel like part of a community of people who are connected. You don't have to feel self-conscious at all; you can let go and connect positively.

The other thing is that I have a friend out of state that I made online, and I love talking to her. The big difference is that with my friends in person, I already know everything about their day-to-day life or whatever drama is going on because I was *there*. I'm already in it, sometimes too much.

On social media, I have someone who is outside of all that. Whatever we talk about, there's no judgment or hard feelings because she's not involved. She's a thousand miles away. I can tell her anything and not worry about it affecting her because she's not in the situation. Having someone outside of our everyday group gives me perspective. I love it.

CHAPTER EIGHT

EXPLORING THE THOUGHTS-FEELINGS-BEHAVIORS CYCLE

Thinking that you have little or no control over your life is stressful and depressing. It can even be stressful and depressing thinking about how stressed and depressed you are. Even if you don't have control over all the events in your life, you can exercise control over your response. It is possible to affect outcomes by preventing self-defeating behavior in response to life occurrences.

The power of positive thinking is certainly not as simple as "thinking good thoughts makes good things happen," as some like to suggest. If only life could be that easy. In fact, it's incredibly unhealthy to insist on having only positive thoughts and permit yourself only positive feelings.

Depression can make it difficult to see how to get out of a painful, repetitive cycle of thoughts and behaviors. Recognizing the thoughts-feelings-behaviors pattern, as illustrated here, can reveal areas where you can break a harmful spiral. *Illustration by Christie Cognevich*

There are no "good" or "bad" emotions—words like "good" and "bad" are lacking and incomplete. Instead of labeling emotions, consider instead how your thought patterns have an impact on your mind and body to change your circumstances. In this case, effective thought patterns can improve a situation even if your emotional state is sad or angry.

Here's how it works.

The mind and body are partners. We've been exploring how the stress response reveals that your emotional and physical experiences are closely related, and how you talk to yourself in your head matters. Here's another way of thinking about it: your thoughts (mental responses), feelings (emotional responses), and behaviors (physical responses) are all tied together.

Thought and behavior patterns are a dance. Each step causes your dance partner to respond; if one dance partner changes how he or she moves, the other adjusts to fit the new pattern.

To demonstrate the thoughts-feelings-behaviors dance, let's say you're trying to earn a spot on the dance team.

I've got pretty good chances, you think to yourself. *I'm giving it my best at practice, and I think I've grown a lot as a dancer.* Because of these positive thoughts, you feel confident and upbeat in the days before tryouts.

Those feelings help you keep steady, clear focus so that you're able to plan out your time well for the next few days, practice well, stay hydrated, and get good sleep. The captain and coach notice how much effort you're putting in at all the practices leading up to the tryouts.

These healthy behaviors, in turn, provoke more positive thoughts. When you're well rested and feeling physically and mentally healthy, you can get out of bed the day of tryouts, stretch, and think to yourself, *I've got this!*

Feeling excited and strong fuels your energy levels, and since you're feeling so confident, your steps are steady and your mind is clear as you perform.

Your improved performance reinforces these positive thoughts about yourself and your abilities. You've just created a healthy looping dance pattern that keeps producing more healthy thoughts, feelings, and behaviors.

The depression loop works the same way, but with unhealthy thoughts, feelings, and behaviors. As the concept of any cycle implies, it's a challenging ride to exit once you're on it.

This time you want to make the dance team, but you tell yourself that you don't have what it takes.

There's no way I'll make it, you tell yourself. *Everyone else is more talented and graceful.*

These thoughts leave you feeling unmotivated, so you skip some practices and feel guilty about it later. Your feelings of guilt and frustration bounce around in your head, keeping you up at night, leading up to the tryouts.

Because you're sleeping poorly at night, you feel sluggish and sleep late. Sleeping late puts you behind schedule on your other responsibilities, so you end up feeling overloaded and behind, reinforcing your negative self-beliefs.

When you finally show up at a practice, you're tired, stressed, and self-conscious about all the other practices you missed. You know the captain and coach have noticed you blowing off practices. You don't know the moves as well as you could. In this exhausted and nervous state, your reflexes are slow and you feel awkward, now reinforcing your original beliefs that everyone else dances better.

Since your self-confidence is so low, you decide it's not even worth going to the tryouts. Now you feel like a quitter. "You're useless," you tell yourself. Self-loathing and depression cycle on and on.

Alternatively, you might tell yourself that everyone else is better, so you have to practice twice as hard. In obsessing over perfection, you might exhaust or injure yourself. Maybe you lose sight of your passion for dance and make something you once enjoyed feel like punishment instead. Your burned-out performance from overdoing it won't compare to performing when you feel healthy, thus reinforcing your negative beliefs about your abilities.

Recognizing how your thoughts, feelings, and behaviors reinforce each other, however, can help you understand and break the cycle. For example, you might have upsetting thoughts without acting on or responding to them. You can have thoughts and emotions without them "having" you and taking control. Recognizing the cycle means you might do something you regret but can avoid letting it throw you into an avoidant or self-loathing mind-set that fuels more destructive behavior. It's okay to feel guilty if you cheated on a test because that guilt can prevent you from doing it again. Here you've recognized your behavior without letting the negative thoughts and feelings it provoked spiral out of control. If you're in the depression loop and don't realize it, those guilty thoughts might turn into deep feelings of shame and self-loathing, which you might try to avoid by faking sick the next time there's a test or bottling them up, causing more distress, and so on.

In the next chapter, we'll explore how to deal with depression without feeling like you have to get rid of your emotions or force positivity that you aren't feeling. Acknowledging an emotional truth—even when that truth is depressed or fearful—is a healthier step forward than pretending it away.

CHAPTER NINE

THE PROBLEM WITH FORCED POSITIVITY

In the previous chapters, we addressed recognizing and tracking your thoughts, feelings, and behaviors often as a way of keeping tabs on your stress and emotional well-being. This chapter goes more in depth with mindfulness strategies once you identify your stressors, struggles, and barriers to getting help. The ultimate goal is not perfection and perfect happiness, but figuring out realistic ways to pursue emotional balance, including building healthier coping skills and working on values-based thinking.

You might experience many barriers in journeying toward improved mental health. Whether your problem is serious, like an abusive relationship, or something more routine like a stressful day at work, these problems can pitch you headfirst into that depression loop where your thoughts, feelings, and behaviors all feed off one another into helpless turmoil. It doesn't have to be that way.

Dealing with depression isn't the same as getting rid of your emotions. We don't want to get rid of emotions—they help us survive. Accepting your emotional truth is part of dealing with depression.

The depression loop is so challenging to overcome in part because we live in a society that encourages positivity over emotional truth. In a 2017 TED talk, psychologist Susan David recalls losing her father at age fifteen, maintaining her high grades, and then receiving praise "for being strong." She believed she was supposed to swallow down the true weight of her grief—and pretend away the terrible emotional and financial upheaval she was witnessing at home. It was only when a

teacher gave David a notebook and encouraged her to write the truth
about her feelings that David felt "invited to show up authentically to
my grief and pain."[1]

David believed that no one wanted to hear about how badly she felt.
She clung to denial and said she was doing okay when people asked. As
a result, forced positivity kept her from healing. Instead of suppressing
our pain, she suggests, we benefit from feeling *all* of our emotions across
a wide range instead of insisting on a rigid "think positive" mind-set.

You might recall in the last chapter, where I mentioned there are
no emotions that are specifically "good" or "bad" because they all have
their purposes. We might think of jealousy as a bad emotion, but within
reason, it can motivate you to achieve more than you might have otherwise managed. We might think of love as a good emotion, but not
every action taken in the name of love is necessarily good or healthy.
(Still regretting that I did all of my boyfriend's chemistry lab reports
in high school in the name of love.) It is only when our emotions no
longer serve their purpose effectively that they become problematic.
Forced positivity is inauthentic, avoidant, and just as problematic as any
so-called bad emotion.

Feeling like no one wants to hear what you're experiencing is heart-
breaking and lonely. Wrestling with your emotions to make them fit
the shape of what you think you "should" feel is an exhausting and
frustrating fight that you can't win. When David surveyed more than
seventy thousand people, at least a third felt self-judgmental about their
feelings of sadness, anger, and grief, or tried to suppress those emotions.
You're probably familiar with being prompted to count your blessings,
put a smile on your face, or look at the bright side, and you've probably
told yourself that you "should" be feeling happier or more grateful for
what you have.

Smiling and basking in the sun with your face turned to the bright
side is wonderful—when you can. When you suppress or ignore what
you're genuinely feeling, however, those emotions don't go away.
Instead, they quietly grow in power. Refusing to acknowledge depression can make its roots grow down deeper. As David points out, trying

to ignore the delicious cake in the refrigerator doesn't make you want it less—it's usually the opposite. Similarly, depression and anxiety can make themselves omnipresent when suppressed.

Why is forced positivity so damaging? David explains that "when we push aside normal emotions to embrace false positivity, we lose our capacity to develop skills to deal with the world as it is, not as we wish it to be." Avoiding disappointment, pain, grief, rage, and fear is impossible. Even the happiest, luckiest, richest people will experience seasons of loss and walk in the shadows for a while.

Studies show that allowing yourself to feel your genuine emotions without judgment won't make you more depressed, even if what you're feeling is one of the "negative" emotions.[2] Recognizing that negative emotions are part of being human and allowing yourself to feel them can pave the way for better well-being.

Accepting the full range of your emotions nonjudgmentally won't *automatically* make you happy, but doing so helps you break free of difficult behavioral-emotional cycles of self-judgment, shame, isolation, and anger that compound and reinforce your initial emotions.

Has there ever been a time when forced positivity or avoiding the full range of your feelings hurt you?

Audrey

My mother died when I was thirteen. In a car accident, so it was very sudden.

It devastated the family. No one knew what to do, how to react. So we didn't. Essentially, we acted like it never happened.

Dad took bereavement leave from work, and our grand-mothers traded weeks staying with us, but otherwise, it was life as usual. My sister (who was six) and I went back to school the day after the funeral. I kept going to play rehearsals and club meetings. Not wanting to be the weird girl with the dead mother, I didn't talk about it with my friends.

After her mother died, Audrey threw herself into various activities and forced positivity, leading her to feel numb and depressed. *Illustration by Kate Haberer*

The only person in my family who talked about it was my maternal grandmother, and her outward displays of grief made me all the more determined to keep everything I was feeling inside.

The denial set off an emotional trip wire in me, and I couldn't access my emotions any longer—sad or happy. And anytime a feeling did slip through, it seemed too big, too scary, so I boxed it up and shoved it out of mind, just like we did with Mom's belongings.

It was years of constant therapy, work, backsliding, and relapsing before I felt like I had made any progress. My family still doesn't talk about what we went through, but I have made long strides in being in touch with my emotions.

Contrary to what I told myself in the past, naming my feelings, being honest with others about how I feel, and communicating my needs has made me smarter, more stable, and focused. I look back in awe, wondering how I survived all those years cut off from myself and remember I almost didn't.

Jael

What I find is that when I want to vent and let myself feel unhappy about something, a lot of my friends and family try to offer advice or fixes. Maybe I'm weird, but most of the time, that doesn't make me feel better at all. It makes me feel pressured to meet their expectations of being all better already.

A close friend once told me that I could find a cloud for every silver lining. That hurt a little bit because he made me sound like a negative person, but I don't think I am. Maybe it's because I'm a sensitive person, but it takes me a little while to get over something—I'm not in a rush about "moving on."

I'm not saying I *don't* want ever to fix whatever my problems are, or that I want to sit and dwell endlessly on bad things. Sometimes I do want their encouragement or advice. But I want to feel like I can be miserable or furious about something without having to jump to make it all better.

When my grandfather died, I was heartbroken. Everyone wants to remember the good. Yes, he lived a good, long life and was pretty healthy until he died in his eighties. Yes, I felt fortunate that I got to have him in my life for as long as I did so that I could know him. Yes, I was lucky enough to visit him in the hospital and have a good conversation with him while he was awake and mentally clear before he died. All of these are good things, and I'm thankful for them.

Losing him was hard, and I needed to feel a lot more than sticking to looking at the bright side. My biological father was an alcoholic who wasn't in the picture, and my stepdad abused me, so my grandfather was the only great man in my life. I needed a lot of time to grieve that. I am grateful for the good things, but I needed to acknowledge that losing him meant losing a really important part of my heart and the only positive, strong male influence I'd ever known. I didn't necessarily want to let it go because to do so quickly, I'd have to stuff it down.

I think taking my time with my sadness helped me in the long run. It sucked when it seemed like friends were sick of hearing that I was sad. But I also found out who was good to talk to in certain situations. I have a friend who always asks me whether I want actual feedback or just someone to listen. Now she's the first one I text when I need to talk.

Also, when I talk to or text my friends, and I want to be able to say what I'm feeling, I'll begin it with something like, "I need to vent so I can feel better. You don't have to give any advice or anything. Is that okay?"

ACCEPTING EMOTIONS TO CREATE CHANGE

Often we think of change as an action, something we need to *do* to make a change happen. However, we all need time and space to process our feelings. Change can also come from the stillness of letting yourself feel—to feel without doing anything at all to make the feeling go away while accepting that just being with the feeling is part of letting it pass.

Interrupting a damaging thoughts-feelings-behaviors cycle begins with the acceptance that thoughts are just thoughts, and feelings are just feelings. You're allowed to have them, no matter how big and unruly and ugly they are. They can't force you to do anything. You don't have to do anything about them, either. There's nothing necessarily wrong with being furious or mortified or terrified or heartbroken. Acceptance is different than resignation and defeat. Acceptance doesn't mean you're helpless to do anything about your emotions. It means you aren't required to *act* on your emotions. Think about the difference.

An acceptance-based response to a range of feelings can build your ability to sit with and ride through discomfort and difficulty. Life comes at us in waves. If we go with our first impulses to act to get rid of a feeling, acting out to escape can often make the problem worse. The same goes for when we get defensive. When you don't feel inconvenienced and harassed by your thoughts and feelings, it's easier to make better choices in response to them. These are just moments, and they come with thoughts and feelings that are just thoughts and feelings. They will pass.

Denial and avoidance of your emotions take effort—it keeps painful things still cycling in your mind and uses up emotional energy. It's okay for thoughts to come through that you may not like or may not be helpful. Suppressing thoughts is like trying to hold a beach ball underwater. They're going to erupt to the surface eventually with greater force, and you'll get unpleasantly splashed in the face as a result. Let the thoughts come through and then float away, just words in your mind that you've had but don't need to act on.

For example, it's possible to have depressed thoughts and feelings without letting them take over and guide your behaviors. The associated behavior response for feelings like sadness, anxiety, fear, guilt, disgust, and embarrassment is generally isolation and avoidance; if you have uncomfortable feelings, you typically try to avoid the cause or push the feelings away. Faking sick to avoid school after an embarrassing rumor will probably cause more problems than it'll solve. Eventually, you'll have to go back to school and face everyone, except now you'll be anxious *and* behind on your work. Distracting yourself from pain by endlessly bingeing on Netflix will also get in the way of doing what you need to do in life. (You can use a distraction as a short-term solution to calm down, but everything in moderation!) Numbing yourself using food, drugs, or alcohol is another incredibly self-destructive form of avoidance. In short, you can have depression without isolation and avoidance having *you*.

You might sometimes get caught up in some unhealthy behaviors. You might not always rely on the best coping skills or make the right choice. Letting yourself have those mistakes without getting too judgmental about them is essential to avoid setting off another depression loop. Of course, it's a delicate balance between letting yourself have some breathing room to trip up sometimes and just making excuses for yourself.

Remember, it's not the feeling itself that's a problem. It's when the behavior responding to the feeling causes problems.

The next time someone tells you to think positively, listen, try to see the love and care behind their intent, and accept that you feel what you feel anyway. Your version of thinking positively is feeling the full range of your emotional truth. You'll get through your difficulties on your timeline.

It's worth saying a second time: a change doesn't have to be an action—it can be merely allowing yourself to be still and live with a big feeling. This will help you ride the waves of discomfort in your life, get past them without avoiding or bottling it up, and eventually become better at handling those life moments.

CHAPTER TEN

EFFECTIVELY DEALING WITH EMOTIONAL DISCOMFORT

Imagine that you have an emotional discomfort cup. It's not a fixed size—some days, all the big cups are dirty, and there are only little cups left, and on better days, you've got your choice of big cups. When your cup is bigger, your capacity for dealing with emotional discomfort is larger. Sometimes your cup is smaller. It happens. Your range of cups can grow with you—you're not stuck with one little cup size forever.

Regardless of your cup's size at the moment, when your distressing thoughts and feelings—sadness, anger, frustration, and so forth—fill up the cup to overflowing, it can be hard to withhold your urge to act on them. Your coping skills protect you by keeping your emotional discomfort cup from hitting overflow.

Some coping techniques distract you so that you don't notice how full your emotional discomfort cup is; they buy time until you're in a better situation or mind-set to pour out a little bit from your cup. Other coping techniques give you enough comfort or pleasure to actively lower your distress level or expand your cup size in the face of problems.

Sometimes, all it takes is a single drop to overflow a cup. If a minor inconvenience overflows your cup, that means your cup wasn't empty to start. You were already at 95 percent full when your snack got stuck in the vending machine, or you misplaced your cell phone, overflowing your cup.

A big problem might not overflow your cup on a good day when you're in a healthy mind-set, but if your cup is already filled with worries, it will. During good times, you might wake well rested with yesterday's discomforts poured out, but during rough times, that may not be the case.

The thoughts-feelings-behaviors loop can be hard to disrupt if your cup is often hovering around crisis levels prompting you to take action to escape the feeling instead of sitting with it. If you've ever noticed yourself or someone you know explode in anger or burst into tears or get suddenly frustrated over something small or seemingly out of nowhere, the cup was already on the verge of overflow.

Keeping track of your emotional discomfort can help you to know when you need to take a moment for yourself or turn to some healthy coping skills before you're in full distress. It's also useful to know where you are starting each day. Do you wake up already feeling tense? What are you carrying over from the previous day? Can you be kinder to yourself?

When the cup reaches its tipping point, it overflows with a tide of other worries and concerns, not just the distressing thoughts directly related to the immediate trigger. This outpouring of other troubles can intensify how depressed, fragile, paralyzed, or furious you're feeling.

Coping trackers like this one can help determine whether your coping strategies are effective or ineffective in lowering your depression and distress. Download a free blank version for you to use on the author's website at christiecognevich.com. *Illustration by Christie Cognevich*

Sometimes we wake up already pretty close to our emotional limits, and other events and interactions throughout the day can make that worse. Distress trackers like this one can help you see whether interactions are helpful or harmful in raising or lowering your emotional distress. Download a free blank version for you to use on the author's website at christiecognevich.com. *Illustration by Christie Cognevich*

Awareness of what you're feeling—especially when you're used to regularly keeping track of the stressors and issues in your life—can help you prevent bringing all the other troubles along for the ride.

COPING SKILLS

Accepting all emotions instead of acting to get rid of "bad" emotions means you might need to look for more coping skills to put in your emotional toolbox.

We need coping skills because while physical and emotional pain differ, the urge to act quickly is the same. When you touch a hot stove, your body's fast-acting response helps you recoil in pain immediately. In protecting yourself from the physical threat of a hot stove, you do need to act on impulse. Individuals with a rare condition who are unable to feel pain frequently injure themselves severely and often because they aren't compelled to pull back from threats. Pausing to think about a burned hand without pulling your hand away will make the situation worse. Emotional pain doesn't follow the same rules of action.

Emotional conditions like depression and anxiety bring a kind of pain that can't be solved on a snap judgment as quickly as removing your hand from the stove. If your childhood was more chaotic, you might be used to continually looking for what's wrong and how to fix it. By surviving to your teenage years, you have proved yourself competent at taking action to ensure physical survival—you have (probably) touched a minimal number of hot stoves, learned how to stay out of the way of potentially dangerous people, and so forth. Just as we learn to act when in danger, we also have to learn *not* to act when we're emotionally strained.

A long-term goal might be to relieve your unhappiness. That may not be immediately possible, especially since depression often has no apparent cause. The goal *right now* might be to tolerate depression, anxiety, or whatever emotional discomfort you're experiencing until you are clearer, calmer, and healthier to take action (or the situation causing the heightened emotion ends). To be clear, that means coping skills are not the same as avoidance.

Throughout your life, you've developed a set of protective emotional skills that shield you when you feel too emotionally hurt, traumatized, or conflicted to process your experiences. They give you a break when what you're feeling is too much to handle all at once or will overflow your cup at that moment. What are those skills? Are they effective? How do you know—how do you feel the difference between before and after you use your coping skills? Now is a good time to reflect on how you process your emotional burdens. Some choices that people use to ease their emotional burden include:

- Responding with sarcasm/humor/joking

- Responding with smiling/laughing

- Not speaking/not participating

- Zoning out/not listening

- Putting up walls/distrust

- Avoiding difficult topics

- Talking to trusted people

- Spending time with friends

- Meditation/breathing exercises

- Napping/sleeping

- Journaling

- Using creativity as an outlet

- Physical activity

- Keeping preoccupied with distractions (from work, hobbies, games, social media)

- Being critical or judgmental (toward self or others)

- Perfectionism

- Self-harm, including cutting or burning

- Numbing through drugs, alcohol, sex, or food (over- or undereating)

- Risk taking/carelessness

- Bullying

- Picking fights/lashing out at others

- Professing hatred, including prejudice/racism/sexism

As you can see, not all of these are the best choices. Some give you space to breathe, but some of these behaviors cruelly push your hurt and anger onto others. Some will make you dishonest to yourself and your loved ones. Some prevent you from feeling. Hurting others won't help you, and not feeling isn't the same as coping.

When one area of your life is falling, can it be useful to focus on your schoolwork as a distraction? Or to pause, take an hour nap, and recharge after a difficult day? Absolutely, but to fixate on schoolwork obsessively or sleep constantly will have negative consequences. A thirty-minute distraction to play a video game that winds your nerves down is healthy. A five-hour avoidance binge isn't healthy—if you always suppress what you're feeling in favor of long-term distractions, those emotions will eventually erupt in unmanageable and destructive ways.

Coping skills aren't one size fits all for every situation. Maybe you got in the habit of deflecting embarrassment or uncertainty with sarcasm. Sarcastically funny ten-year-olds can be hilarious and seem witty beyond their years, garnering you positive attention and better self-esteem. However, five years down the line, maybe your sarcasm has started getting you in trouble in class or with your parents. Now, your sarcasm comes across less like wit and more like a class distraction or disrespect. While your perfectionism might have helped you take pride in your work even when your self-esteem was low, has it started leaving you feeling overly self-critical and inadequate lately?

If you find that you often need to cope with the consequences of your coping skills, your skills are raising your emotional discomfort level instead of lowering it, and they may not be beneficial. Some important coping skills may yield brief uncomfortable results—like having a tough conversation—but shouldn't provoke frequent problems. It's worth repeating—if your coping methods produce results that you need to cope with, ask yourself with honesty: Are they pushing your emotional discomfort cup closer to overflow instead of lowering it? Did the result make more problems or ease your burden somewhat? If it caused more problems, can you be honest with yourself about whether those problems were necessary hurdles to a healthier, better life?

As you can see, there aren't always perfect fixes—you might outgrow your old methods or start using them unhealthily. Awareness not just of your difficulties but whether the result of how you coped is effective or ineffective can help you in discovering what might be adding to your emotional burden instead of subtracting from it. Like using the other trackers, having awareness is the first step to seeing which behaviors are really improving your life and which are unnecessarily complicating it.

Remember, coping with your difficulties takes up energy. If coping helps at the moment but creates long-term problems, you might be spending energy on something that's draining you.

CHAPTER ELEVEN

EXPLORING HEALTHY RELATIONSHIPS

Friends, Peers, Family Issues, and Social Isolation

Effectively dealing with depression can be doubly difficult if you're involved in difficult, dangerous, or toxic relationships with any family, friends, or significant others. Relationships have a substantial impact on your emotional health—helping you up *or* keeping you down. One in three American adolescents has experienced physical, sexual, emotional, or verbal abuse from a dating partner—and *half* of the adolescents who have experienced rape and dating violence attempt suicide.[1] For this reason, exploring your healthy or unhealthy relationship dynamics can have a huge impact on helping you take care of your mental health.

Fighting isn't necessarily unhealthy. Everyone has conflicts with others in their lives, whether it's an active fight or just a passive situation where two people don't mesh all the time. We need to disagree to see broader viewpoints and explore our own. Abusive relationships force an unhealthy thoughts-feelings-behaviors cycle and foster shame, self-loathing, and self-blame. Similarly, a toxic relationship that isn't *explicitly* abusive but is unhealthy can keep you always feeling needy for someone, under obligation to someone who needs you, or even both.

It can be difficult to distinguish normal, healthy conflicts from a truly toxic dynamic. This is especially true if you're in a relationship where you don't necessarily feel physically threatened. A relationship that often leaves you emotionally destabilized and drained can also be incredibly unhealthy for you.

If a partner or friend keeps you from doing things you like or doesn't allow you to spend time with other friends, you might be feeling emotionally unsafe. Often having to tiptoe around to not anger or offend someone is a state of feeling emotionally unsafe. Sometimes you will choose to make sacrifices for partners and friends; often, you will try to avoid upsetting partners and friends, and this is normal. If you are *under pressure* to satisfy another individual and don't feel safe sometimes making other choices, this is unhealthy.

You deserve to feel physically and emotionally safe—and of course, others should feel physically and emotionally safe around you.

One useful way of thinking about relationships is that everyone has fundamental human rights, including in a relationship. The organization loveisrespect (loveisrespect.org), the first 24/7 American helpline for teenagers in abusive relationships, has many resources about healthy relationships and understanding your rights. They point out that in any dating or friendship relationship, all individuals deserve:

- To feel safe and respected

- To live free from violence and all abuse—physical, sexual, emotional, verbal

- To have personal space to be with family and friends, as well as to do what you enjoy, without a jealous or controlling partner

- To have privacy, both online and off

- To have the decision-making ability over who you date or not

- To have the decision-making ability over your sexual choices

- To be able to say no (or change your mind if you've said yes before) to anything, including sex, drugs and alcohol, or a relationship

- To have the decision-making ability to leave any relationship you don't want, isn't right, or isn't healthy

Many of these rights are valid for family relationships as well. There are *no* exceptions to feeling safe, respected, and able to live free of violence and abuse.

One key difference in relationship rights with your parents/guardians is their ultimate responsibility to protect you and provide for your ongoing safety. Their healthy respect for your individuality and growing maturity can and should be balanced with their reasonable and important concerns about your privacy and decision-making.

This balance is the big distinction between a controlling and abusive parent who makes you feel *unsafe* versus a parent who keeps an eye on your social media, who you're with, and where you're going. The latter might bother you but not make you feel endangered.

In a healthy parenting situation, you have the right not to be neglected, which means you have the right to your parents/guardians caring and *not* letting you do everything you want. With your parents/guardians and your family, you deserve:

- To feel safe and respected and not be placed in situations where you might be unsafe or disrespected

- To live free from violence and all abuse—physical, sexual, emotional, verbal—and not be placed in danger of violence or abuse

- To be with family and friends, as well as to do what you enjoy—within reasonable time frames with trustworthy individuals

- To not feel obligated to parent or provide for your parents or guardians

- To have a healthy understanding of privacy being modeled by parents/guardians observing you

- To have your parents/guardians model healthy behaviors about deciding life choices—including providing for your safety through some expectations and restrictions on your behavior

Remember, there is never *any* circumstance in which you should feel unsafe or endangered mentally, physically, or sexually by anyone, whether they are family, friend, or stranger.

Depression can leave you vulnerable. Finding a healthy support system with people you can trust and talk to is a big part of your emotional health. Consider the individuals in your life who are helping you feel stable, safe, and secure. Are there any who don't? Be honest with yourself as you evaluate the relationships in your life.

If you are experiencing abuse, aren't sure if what you're experiencing is abuse, or have questions or concerns about your relationships, there are resources and advocates out there for you. Do you have questions or need to check in with someone? Do you need help?

There are many safe, confidential, free, immediate options available for you to talk, text, or chat with someone if you are concerned, confused, or have questions or need to talk about your relationship dynamics.

- **In the United States,** call loveisrespect at 1-866-331-9474. There are options for Spanish speakers and the deaf/hard of hearing. There is also a live online chat available with advocates on their website at loveisrespect.org. If you feel more comfortable texting, text LOVEIS to 22522.

- **In the United Kingdom,** call the National Domestic Abuse Helpline at 0808 2000 247.

- **In Canada,** there is a range of options available for you, depending on your province. The Ending Violence Association of Canada has a list available on their website at http://endingviolencecanada.org/getting-help/.

- **In Australia**, call 1800RESPECT at 1800 737 732. There is also an online chat service on their website at https://www.1800respect .org.au/.

HEALTHIER COMMUNICATION

To achieve many of these relationship rights, feeling open and safe to communicate with others is essential. Communication keeps you on the same page with your loved ones—your expectations, needs, feelings, and vice versa. Communication means talking about things that might be bothering you, not holding things in or bottling feelings up, but also means sharing in the lighthearted times, too—being able to laugh together or share memories. Open communication is open in the good times and the bad.

Healthy communication involves compromise and respect. The best relationships involve both individuals expressing themselves in moments of strength *and* weakness, and neither individual sacrificing essential parts of themselves. You should be able to share what you think, feel, and desire, and vice versa, without the fear of being shut down, rejected, or silenced. Communication is not about avoiding all disagreements, but building room in the relationship to share thoughts while the other listens.

When you're feeling distressed or depressed, communication can feel difficult, especially if you lack words to explain what you're thinking and feeling. It can be useful to write out your thoughts beforehand then take a little time to rethink what you want to say before you communicate. Taking time can prevent you from speaking in the heat of the moment, saying something you don't mean, or experiencing the frustration of not knowing how to explain what you mean.

Talk with others about their relationships—family, friendships, romantic. What works in their communication habits? What's frustrating? Even in the healthiest of relationships, there will occasionally be communication breakdowns. How do others overcome them? How did they deal with unhealthy communication situations and toxic relationships? Conversation builds the skills in your emotional toolbox.

RELATIONSHIP STRUGGLES

Just like it's impossible to cover every stressor, it's impossible to capture the incredible emotional complexity of every kind of relationship. This book will stick to some common, broad categories like friends and family. In some cases, there is a positive resolution, and in some cases, the difficulties are ongoing.

Let's hear from some people about the relationships they've had and how they impacted their emotional balance.

FRIENDS

How have difficulties with your friends impacted you?

Audrey

One consistent difficulty I've had with friends is the introvert/extrovert struggle.

I am a true introvert, and much prefer spending time one-on-one with friends than going to large group gatherings, and even then, I don't want to see my friends *too* often. I need to spend a lot of time alone.

That's what makes me happy until my extrovert friends would make me feel bad about it. They come from a good place; spending lots of time with lots of people makes them happy, and since that's not what I'm doing, I must not be happy, so they'll "adopt" me. Yes, the word "adopt" has been used on me multiple times.

Usually, they figure out pretty quickly that I *am* happy, I don't need their help, and I can be more of a person and less of a project.

One friend was different. I'll call her Mary. She had "adopted" me almost as soon as I got to college, and we were both theater majors, so there were parties all the time.

Our relationship progressed as they usually do: I'd finally relent and go to a party, not enjoy it, which made her all the more determined to mold me in her image. Unlike past friends, she never caught on that I was happy the way I was.

I really liked her, and we were both stage managers, so we spent *a lot* of time together working on theater shows.

It fell apart after about two years. I was stage managing a huge musical; Mary wasn't working on the show. I had no time in my day—I was in class right up until rehearsal, which took up the entire evening/night; I usually got out around midnight. So I was exhausted, stressed, and (though I didn't realize it at the time) depressed, so my desire to be alone was even higher than usual.

She would. Not. Stop. Calling. Me. Take a hint, girl—if you're leaving messages and I'm not calling back, stop calling!

I was so angry she was adding to my stress. She was also a stage manager. We'd worked together before. She knows how the show takes up your entire life until it closes. Her calling and me ignoring her went on for weeks.

Eventually, she left an extremely angry, yell-y voicemail, and I was done. When I got out of rehearsal, I sent her a breakup email. It was brief, but the only line I remember is, "I believe our time is best spent pursuing other friendships."

We never spoke again.

I don't regret "breaking up" with her. I liked her, but we just wanted different things out of a friendship.

I do regret how I broke up with her, though. I wish I had talked to her when I first started the show that drove us apart when she first started calling all the time. I could have told her, "I miss you, but I'm not going to have any time until the show closes. Let's catch up then," instead of completely ignoring her because "she should know what my life is like."

That cold, clinical email I sent—from her perspective, I ghosted her for six weeks and then said, essentially, "Never talk to me again." That's not what I meant, but it's how I felt at the time. If I had stated my needs earlier, I likely wouldn't have had to do a hard break, and we'd drift apart naturally, in a less hurtful way.

Cailyn

The transition between elementary school and high school was rough for me because I had a friend group that I'd known all growing up in elementary school, so we tried to stick together when we moved to a new school.

I used to play baseball, pitcher and center field, but when I got to high school, I took a break to focus on my grades for a little bit. I didn't have a team anymore, so it was important for me to have some friends, and I was shifting my interests a little from athletics to film production and art.

My friends and I were all sticking to each other because it was hard going from a small school to a big school with over two thousand students. At my school, there are a few places where you can eat lunch inside or outside. We always tried to cluster together in our little lunch group.

I was *so* bored at lunch while they talked. It was like we weren't clicking anymore. My friends would talk about the things they were doing after school, football games, or whatever, and I had absolutely nothing to contribute. So, I just never talked.

I felt safe with them. They knew me, and I knew them. What if I moved lunch groups, and I went away from what I knew was safe?

One day I joined a new lunch group and sat somewhere else. *What if they think I'm weird? What if they think I'm stupid?* I was so worried. And I didn't know how to talk to them or contribute to the conversation. So again, I was sitting there saying nothing.

A few times, my old friends were confrontational about it. "Why are you moving lunch groups? What's your problem?"

Writing in a journal helped me during that time sometimes because I got my fears out, and then I was okay. Sometimes I would have no motivation to journal because I didn't feel like crying, and I knew if I wrote it out, I was going to cry.

I made new friends and clicked with my new group. They know me and accept me. There will be days I get so insecure that it's almost scary. I'm so stuck in my head, and I don't know how to talk to people. I feel so out of it that I'm like, *I don't even feel like myself and I can't even talk.* But my friends get it. We're just sitting next to each other and not even talking and it's cool.

Austin

I had a friend that did musical theater together with me, and she would direct a lot of those productions. You're bound to get close to people that are in the shows with you, and it was wonderful.

There's this old saying I heard that "correction does much; encouragement does everything," and my friend was a corrector, not an encourager. I think that, mixed with a little bit of jealousy on her part, just turned it into a very manipulative friendship.

If I didn't respond to her texts in a certain amount of time, or if I wasn't around on the weekend, she'd get very upset about it.

There are people in this world that have a pure light to them when you meet them. She was one of these people, and she had the brightest light. I think her problem was she also had a lot of demons, and she didn't face them, and so she projected them onto me.

It could be anything from her having a bad day to her broken fingernail, and it would be projected on me.

It got to the point when she was directing me in a show onstage, and she said in front of the entire cast that I wasn't good enough. She'd do things like that, jabs that she knew would hurt me.

She was sitting in the front row of the theater one time, and I was onstage right in front of her. Because she didn't like the way I was walking onstage, she took a ruler and hit it on the stage and cracked it in front of the entire cast.

I started doing a lot of self-evaluation. One of the moments where I realized this was a manipulative, toxic friendship was when she said that the reason why she was so hard on me was because I "never experienced tough love" as she did.

Around the same time, she and one of our other friends weren't getting along anymore. Once she wasn't getting along with him, no one else in the friend group was allowed to get along with him.

That's when my gut was telling me that something wasn't right, that this wasn't a healthy friendship to be in with her.

PEERS

How have your peer relationships, including peer pressure or bullying, impacted you?

Kaitlynn

Last year, which was my first year of high school, there was a girl I was terrified of—I'm going to call her E. She was always mean, but I also sort of wanted her to like me.

She and I had a physical science class together. We experimented in class, making something called elephant's toothpaste, which makes this giant foamy eruption like a toothpaste volcano. You make it by mixing hydrogen peroxide, dish soap, yeast, and water.

E was in my group when we did it, and she kept pressuring me to taste the elephant's toothpaste. She kept saying how *she* was going to take some home and do an experiment on herself and eat it to see what would happen. E kept bothering me to do it, to eat a little bit of it.

I don't know why I did it. It was foolish, but I was scared of E, so I ate just a tiny bit of it. I can't believe I did that stupid thing.

After that, I just avoided her altogether, stopped talking to her, and unfollowed her on all social media. I had to step back. I think I'm pretty good at giving people second chances and have even made friends with people who were kind of mean last year who've changed a lot this year, but I just had to step back from E.

E was also in my homeroom, and she was always trying to pick fights with people. She would be yelling and throwing thumbtacks at another girl. It didn't take long for the counselors and the school principal to step in.

She's also been put in different classes than people she was fighting with and picking on. That's not scary; that's just sad.

This year, we're cheerleaders together. We had a cheerleader meeting to plan a special activity we're doing and design the papier-mâché costumes we're making. She came up to me and acted like she wanted to talk to me about the activity.

Kaitlynn was intimidated by a girl into tasting the science experiment, but is no longer intimidated by her. *Illustration by Kate Haberer*

I was a little confused, but she pulled me aside, and then instead of talking about the plans, E was like, "Why don't you like me?" She seemed sad about it.

Now that I'm looking back, I think she wants to be liked even though she was mean to everyone. She takes everything way too far for attention.

I'm not intimidated or afraid of her anymore; I don't want to be around her. I feel sorry for her because a lot of people don't want to be around her.

Austin

A cousin of mine went to the same high school as me, and we're both very loud people, but in different ways. Since we live in a small town that's about thirty-five minutes away from school, we would all take a bus in the morning to get there.

There's just one bus, and there was a waiting room. Between the waiting hours after school—because you had to wait for everybody to get out of their extracurriculars—and then in the morning on the bus on the way, I would get bullied.

We ended up having what was like a two-year-long feud. We couldn't stand each other, wouldn't talk to each other at Christmas, and he was always in my face picking on me on the bus.

I think a lot of it had to do with what his parents were dealing with—money ordeals and family drama—and I think his parents said things to him, which got taken out on me. Since then, I think a lot of the things he said and did were probably not about hate; they were about hurt and pain. I try to remember that whenever somebody directs something at me. It never has anything to do with me. I'm just an easy target.

There were some issues with peer pressure also. I'm not big on drinking because alcoholism runs in my family. I've seen two older siblings go to rehab for alcohol and drug use. A lot of people I hang out with would want to drink, and they'd be like, "Oh, you would be more fun if you drank!" Um, you know my family has struggled with that, right?

I felt like a drag because I didn't want to drink, and that was something that kind of stuck out and was mentioned a lot. Why can't I be fun sober? You know, it's fine if other people want to drink or smoke or do whatever, but that's not me.

Emma

Sometimes it's the truth that kids are mean, and then I've come to realize they're mean and they don't even know what they're saying sometimes.

In PE class, we were all lined up sitting cross-legged on the gym floor, waiting for the coach to take roll. This guy Alex was walking by. He's just this goofy guy who says and does random things. He's not mean at all, just kind of says whatever he thinks and doesn't have a filter.

Alex was messing around, and he nudged my leg while I was sitting. I guess because of the way I was sitting—let's be honest, I'm not the thinnest—it jiggled my legs. In front of *everyone* in the gym, he announces, "When you hit her thigh, the other one jiggles!" Great. Thanks, Alex! Totally appreciated.

It was like he didn't even expect that it was going to embarrass me or upset me. It's one of those things where people are just jerks to each other, and they don't even stop to think about what they've said or why.

I'm not saying that there aren't people who aren't actively trying to hurt others. There's a guy who rode my bus who made it his mission to make me miserable just because he thought it was funny. I'm the last stop before the bus takes us to school, so basically, I always have to sit wherever there's space. That usually means I'm squeezed in on the edge of a seat because the bus is full, or I'm stuck next to someone that no one else wants to sit with.

Which means I'm the one who has to sit next to this guy all the time. I'm going to call him Matt. At first, I was kind of impressed and intimidated by Matt because he's a grade or two older than me, and he's in a band. In the beginning, I wanted him to think I was cool.

It is my genetic fortune that everyone in my family is ridiculously pale skinned and dark haired. I won the genetic lottery. I probably have a perfectly normal amount of hair on my arms, but the hair is dark, and the skin is lily white, so my arm hair is noticeable.

I would not have said it was noticeable a couple of years ago because I certainly never noticed or cared about my arm hair until I had to sit with Matt on the bus.

Every time he saw me, he brought it up. The hair on my arms was not the topic I thought I was going to hear about daily. I pretty much wanted to die every time I got on the bus, and there he was, and there was the only empty seat right next to him.

I tried so hard to ignore it as it went on for a while, but one day in the shower, while I was shaving my legs, I shaved my arms, too.

He noticed immediately, and he made fun of me as loudly as possible for having shaved my arms.

That was the first and last time I ever shaved my arms.

It didn't matter if my arms were hairy, and it didn't matter if they weren't hairy. Matt is a jerk either way.

FAMILY ISSUES

How have difficulties in your family relationships impacted you?

Austin

My parents divorced when I was three, and my mom married my stepfather when I was four. Since that's all I've ever really known in terms of family dynamics, the biggest upheaval in the family for me wasn't the divorce; it was the huge emotional impact in my living situation when I was about twelve.

My mom has two sisters, and one of the two—not the one I'm closest with—moved in with us with her three children. It was my mom, my stepdad, my aunt, my four siblings and me, and then my three cousins all under one roof.

Now, we do have a pretty big house, but it's not that big. To accommodate eight kids, we were all just piled on top of each other and sharing rooms.

My aunt came from a bad relationship that involved a lot of drugs, a lot of abuse, her getting beat up, and her children saw a lot of that.

When they came, they brought a lot of that emotional turmoil and trauma with them. That spilled over to all of us.

While I was always a pretty mature kid, it was a lot to deal with having all these new people in the house and some pretty dark things being talked about and going on around me.

I'd come home and hear about how this one was doing drugs, and this one got arrested. It was around that time that two of my four siblings were having some trouble too. My older brother and then my older sister both ended up in rehab a few years apart from each other. They both struggled with addiction. That was something that made me lose my innocence, watching that unfold.

What helped me at that time was not being home at my mom's house. Since my parents were divorced, I had two homes. My father's home was a lot less chaotic.

The downside to that is that at my dad's house, I didn't necessarily get attention. As a guide fisherman, my dad works from five in the morning to five in the afternoon. Then when he gets home, he's tired, and he goes to take a shower and goes to bed. It was less turbulent there, but it was also way less nurturing.

Kaitlynn

A few years back, my dad announced to my mom that he didn't love her anymore.

It was a horrible time. My parents almost got divorced, but they worked it out. So to kind of keep things pleasant and romantic, they go on date nights. Everything *looks* okay with them.

It's always in the back of my head now: *Is he just faking?* Because my mom makes more money than he does, and I wonder if that has something to do with him staying with her. She's amazing, and she doesn't deserve how my dad treated her.

Whenever he goes off on her and is yelling, I'm just waiting and wondering if he's going to leave.

Those anxieties show up in my sleep a lot. I know I don't get enough sleep because I stress and worry about things so much. The other night I dreamed that our house got robbed, and it was my dad secretly helping the robbers take from my mom and me.

Jael

I was four when my mom got remarried. One of my earliest memories of my stepdad is within a couple of weeks of them getting married.

I'd been eating Cheetos and got some orange smudges on the wall or something. He was *furious*. I was a really sensitive kid. I don't know if I'd ever been punished before besides just getting fussed at here and there. If I had, it wasn't big enough to register on my memory, and I thought telling stories to my stuffed animals was the height of excitement, so I didn't exactly get up to a lot of trouble.

I got some Cheetos dust on something, and he spanked me and told me to kneel in the corner with my hands behind my back. I remember I was inconsolable.

I knew I had done something awful to get hit and then for the punishment to not even be over. I don't know how long I had to kneel in the corner, but that was the first time of many years of corner kneeling. When I was "really" bad—according to my stepdad—I had to kneel on my hands. If I got in trouble while we were in the car, I had to sit on my hands until we could get home where I could kneel in the corner.

Whenever I was especially upset about having to kneel, my stepdad would tell me that when he was little, he had to kneel on rice, so he was *generous* by not using rice.

There was a lot of corner kneeling in my childhood, years and years of it. Everything set him off. I remember one time he flew into a rage because I had automatically assumed that the toy in my box of cereal belonged to me without asking him permission to have it. Since he had paid for the box of cereal, the toy was *his*.

In retrospect, this kind of ridiculousness might make a funny movie about an overgrown man-child played by Will Ferrell, but not so funny when you're four or five, and this is your actual life.

I guess some kids would toughen up, but I never grew a thick skin. I started sensitive, and I stayed sensitive, so I just cried and cried every time and never really managed to figure out how to avoid his anger. I'm glad I stayed "soft," so to speak.

His cruelty hurt me, but I tried hard not to let it change the heart I had inside of me.

It escalated and escalated. When my mom wasn't around, he was physically abusive. He started sexually abusing me when I was ten. My mom had no clue what was going on; he was so good at hiding everything. I was afraid to go home. I was afraid to sleep. I did everything I could do to hide inside of myself, not be too loud or too noticeable or draw any attention to myself or my body. I never felt safe.

I kept my mouth shut for most of my childhood because I was so afraid of what he would do if I told anyone. He'd threatened to hurt my mom if I ever told, and I knew he could do it. I didn't think anyone would believe me anyway. I was just a kid, a weird, broken, messed-up kid.

When I first told someone, I thought I'd made a huge mistake—I'd reached out because I just wanted to confide in someone. I'd been so alone for so long with all of my secrets and shame and depression. I didn't expect anything to come of it. I didn't think they were going to do anything about it.

They took me to the police, and I had to talk to the detectives, and I was so, so scared. It's tough for me to talk about everything that happened over the next few months, but I'm so glad I told someone.

It wraps up very simply. My stepdad went to prison, and I went to therapy, and everything changed for the better.

I still struggle with depression and anxiety, but I feel safe now. I can go home and go to bed and not live in the constant shadow of fear and shame.

Emma

My mom and dad divorced when I was still a baby. I don't remember that part, but it was a bitter divorce because my dad was irresponsible, didn't pay child support, and would skip visiting when he was supposed to.

My older brother was old enough to remember, so it impacted him a lot more to get ready and get all excited to see our dad, and then have our dad fail to show up.

My mom was upset about how it was affecting my brother to be let down like that all the time, so she told our dad that unless he was going to show up, she wasn't going to let him make arrangements to pick us up. He could stop by and visit us, but he couldn't make big plans to do stuff if he wasn't going to follow through.

Again, I don't remember this happening, but in response, our dad came over to visit, took my brother, and climbed out the bathroom window with him. It was a pretty terrifying day for my mom and grandparents, but they found my dad at his grandma's house with my brother.

As you can imagine, there were no more dad visits after that.

What I do remember well is when I was a little older, we ran into him at the mall. It had been a long time since he'd seen us. He asked my mom if he could take us to the toy store in the mall, and she said okay even though she was scared he'd try to take us.

He took us in there, and he asked me what I wanted, and there was a Barbie that I'd been dreaming of having. It had this cool skirt that you could decorate. I was a kid, so I thought he was asking because he was going to buy it for me right then. He told me that he would get it for me one day and then brought us back to my mom—who, by the way, had been freaking out the whole time thinking he might kidnap us.

I was so, so, so upset and angry! I was probably about six, and I didn't understand why he asked me what I wanted and then *didn't get it*. There was some hurt fury there.

I remember my mom and grandma trying to explain that he probably didn't have the money, but he *wanted* to get me something, and that's what mattered. That didn't comfort me because, again, little kid mentality. It was this huge letdown.

In the end, I made such a big deal out of it that my grandma on my mom's side ended up buying it for me. I feel bad about that now because it comes across as so bratty, but I hadn't seen my father in so long, and I thought he was going to get me a gift. Little kids look for love in materialistic ways sometimes.

After that, my mom was extremely paranoid that we might accidentally run into him. She was glad he hadn't kidnapped us at that time but was convinced that he might try it again. She banned everyone in my family from taking us to our dad's "side" of town. We couldn't go to the mall or restaurants or anything like that on that side of the town because she was so scared. We didn't go back to that part of the town again until I was like twelve or thirteen.

In retrospect, I feel bad for him now. My mom says he didn't know how to be a father, and I think that's probably pretty accurate.

SOCIAL ISOLATION

How has social isolation and distance from others impacted you?

Austin

My internal struggle hasn't been about being gay but about feeling alone. Just thinking, *I gotta overcome it, I gotta overcome it, I gotta overcome it*. What are the odds of me not surviving? They felt high.

It would have been easy to give in to other people's ridiculous mind-sets of "you can only be one thing, and that's it." It would've been easy for me to do that, give up, and not want to go on with

life anymore. What you have to remember at the end of the day—
and I *didn't* remember this, so this might be a little hypocritical—
but to remember you're not alone.

I *thought* I was alone, but, one thing that I can for sure say now,
is that nobody is alone. Even when you are, when you're by yourself, you're still not alone. You've got yourself on your shoulder. You
always have your mind. You can always rely on yourself.

It would have helped me a few years back to know I wasn't alone.
I think that would have been the biggest thing to help me—knowing
that somewhere, could be a thousand miles east or west, some people
support me, who love me, and who will want to help me.

I think the first time I found a supportive community probably was the first time I started doing theater. You find a group that
wants to be around you, one that enjoys your company, and then
there's a love there that's like no other.

I wish I could tell myself that when you find your people, you
feel it. Even if they're not your people for the rest of your life necessarily, but if they're your people, they're your people at that time.
Sometimes you have to work through trusting them, but if there's
something in your gut that says, *Maybe I can confide in these friends,*
don't fight that feeling.

Alyssa

Because of my health issues, I'm usually not allowed to participate
in school activities or events like assemblies and pep rallies.

We also have special events where each grade goes on an overnight weekend retreat together, and we bunk in shared cabins. The
school administration didn't allow me to spend the night because of
my health issues. I was also told by some people that I shouldn't go
because I'd be a burden to the girls who would have to share a room
with me overnight and would make them worry about having to
take care of me if I got sick or passed out.

I was allowed to go during the day; then, my mom had to drive
out to the campground to pick me up while everyone else stayed.

The feeling of that isolation and being left out is one of the worst parts of my health. I could deal with health problems, but the way I worry about burdening others all the time is miserable.

Jael

My stepdad's abuse forced me into social isolation.

One time when I was about thirteen, we had a half day at school for the teachers to have professional development. I was looking forward to being home alone because that was the only time I felt free and safe.

He wasn't at work like I thought he was going to be. I was always terrified to be home alone with him because I never knew what he was going to say or do to me.

He ended up hitting me in the face and splitting my lip open that day. I knew my mom and my friends were going to want to know what happened when they saw it, so I made up a story about how I'd tripped on the rug and hit my mouth on the coffee table.

Deep down, I desperately hoped that someone would call me out and say that it looked like someone had hit me. I'd faked being fine for so long, and no one questioned it. That made me curl up inside of myself more. It felt like even when there was a red flag, no one noticed, so I was just more convinced that no one would ever see I needed help.

I realize now that wasn't the case. I am surrounded by so much love and support. I could have talked to anyone. I'm not alone at all. I don't blame myself for not having spoken up sooner, but I hope others know there is help out there.

PART III

RESOLUTION AND RESOURCES

CHAPTER TWELVE

MAINTAINING YOUR LIGHT

Depression is not necessarily overcome once. Recovery is an ongoing state. What can you do daily to help maintain better mental health? Self-care is a daily process.

Self-care is a popular term these days. Staying hydrated is self-care. Treating yourself with purchases and physical pampering to allowing yourself some downtime to do something purely for fun can be self-care if it doesn't go overboard. Sometimes it's turning off your phone or getting offline when you need to unplug. There's no one right way to do self-care. Going out might recharge your batteries, or staying in with a book might recharge your batteries. Journaling can be self-care. Your self-care depends on you.

The act of doing something for yourself is far more critical than the length of time you do it. For example, setting attainable goals like journaling for five minutes a day is far more realistic than journaling for an hour a day. Setting small but manageable goals can help you from feeling overwhelmed when you need to conserve your mental and emotional resources for other things.

No goal is too small. Small goals are helpful because they're fully achievable. For a long time, one of my daily goals was to take a shower. During a time when I was sad, stressed, and overwhelmed, the thought of tackling big projects left me feeling drained and paralyzed. When I knew I was going to have to do something that would take thought, all my thought processes ran dry. Thinking of tackling anything that might *not* be finished that day was an impossible prospect. Taking a shower was doable, a goal achieved for the day.

Building and maintaining effective habits for better mental health won't jump-start you into happiness overnight. There are days when you'll forget to practice some of your coping skills and days when you'll realize you didn't handle difficult moments as well as you could. Doing what you can to practice better thought patterns and coping skills will make them easier to remember and more effective in your day-to-day life. Practice means building up your ability to do something over time; the same is necessary for life habits.

Every single time you practice a healthy emotional skill successfully, the odds that you'll do it well again next time goes up just a little. The following are skills to practice for better emotional and mental health.

EVALUATE AND IDENTIFY YOUR HIDDEN EMOTIONS

Knowing your feelings is a skill. Before you can work with your feelings, you need awareness of what's bothering you. It may not always be what the immediate trigger seems to be. What's underneath your surface emotions? Taking the time for self-care and then evaluating a situation when you feel a little better can be helpful. One healthy practice is to journal emotions: keep track of your feelings and then evaluate the feeling that's hiding underneath. A five-minute daily journal covering your emotions can be very useful.

- What happened today?

- What was my emotional response to it?

- Is there any other feeling underneath that? Why might I have those feelings?

- How can I take care of the vulnerable part of myself having those hidden feelings?

Anger is often described as a protective, secondary emotion. Sometimes, when you feel angry, your anger is serving as a shield, protecting you from the painful feelings lurking underneath. Your anger serves a productive purpose in this case, letting you choose the moment when you feel like you can be vulnerable and peek underneath the anger.

Do you struggle to communicate when you're angry or in emotional distress? It's possible to set up your brain for useful communication habits just by taking a little time and care to step back from that thoughts-feelings-behaviors loop. Speaking is an action, so pausing to process your feelings and recognizing you don't have to act on them or say anything that comes to mind is a great habit.

It's fine to be angry. Your anger can serve a healthy and productive purpose by shielding you when you need it. You don't need to *act* on the anger. The anger itself is fine and even useful. Now pause and evaluate it. What's causing you those feelings?

Don't wait too long to think about your hidden emotions, but do wait until you feel safe and secure to check in with yourself. Do some self-care; then take the time to breathe and acknowledge the full range of your emotions.

For example, your friend agrees to go with you to an event so you won't be alone and then bails on you at the last minute. You might feel angry that your friend is ditching you, or that he waited until the last minute to tell you, or that he does this all the time and you feel like you're drifting apart.

Check in with yourself within a day or two after you unwind a little. *What's on my mind? What am I feeling? Is there anything underneath that feeling? If I feel angry, is that anger protecting me from the full weight of some other emotion?*

It's very likely that while you're also angry, your anger might be protecting you from feelings of hurt, fear, and insecurity. *He hurt me. What if he and I are drifting apart? I feel like he's continually blowing me off lately. Does he not like me anymore? Am I too needy? Did I do something wrong? Why has he started acting like a jerk to me? Do I deserve it?*

Let yourself feel that disappointment or anything else you may be feeling. How can you express that to your friend instead of blowing up or giving him the cold shoulder? Maybe your friend dropped the ball on you for good reasons, or perhaps you are drifting apart. It's only in talking to him in a clearer state of mind that you can determine that.

"When you didn't go with me to the party yesterday, I felt sad that it seems like we're drifting apart," is a much more effective way of identifying what you're feeling and communicating it than telling your friend while you're angry that he's a selfish jerk.

COPING AHEAD

When depressed, we can often spend our time thinking about the worst-case scenario that might happen. Or if the worst-case scenario *has* happened, we replay it in our minds over and over again.

Neither is useful, but coping ahead of time can be highly helpful. Start coping ahead of time for likely situations. There's little healthy use in expending time, energy, and emotions over things that are unlikely, while it is worth thinking about circumstances that are likely to occur.

Coping ahead isn't the same as worrying. Pretending that possible negative outcomes won't happen or avoiding thinking about it at all can leave you unprepared if that outcome does occur. Hanging all your hopes on the single good outcome is rarely effective. In coping ahead, consider visualizing helpful response scenarios. The key is dealing with life flexibly rather than worrying about how life might turn out wrong.

For example, you are invited to go on a beach trip with your friend's family, and you want to go. Deep down, you know that your family can't afford to pay for your travel, and it's highly unlikely you'll be able to go. An ineffective way of thinking about it might be to picture all the activities you'll miss out on: swimming, surfing, late-night hangouts. This thinking will only build your depression and feelings of missing out.

An effective way of coping in advance might be to accept your disappointment and then plan out what you'll do instead, like some fun activities closer to home with other friends. Alternatively, you might recognize that it's disappointing while also strategizing about what you can do to earn some of the money you need to go. Or you can make plans for what you'll do the next time you get invited, so you know that next time you will be able to go.

CHAPTER THIRTEEN

EXPLORING SELF-CARE

Focusing on self-care is not quite the same as what we think of as "self-help." Self-help is a broad term, but in short, any product focused on personal improvement and growth falls under the heading of self-help—How to be a better friend; How to achieve success; How to be more organized; How to be happy. Self-help exists as an *eleven-billion-dollar industry*—from YouTubers to Instagram influencers to BuzzFeed articles to movies and books—because people are willing to spend money to find happiness for themselves and their loved ones. Similar to the problem with advice, the problem with self-help is that a lot of it—not all, but a fair amount—is grounded in quick fixes, suggesting that if you try hard enough and do the right things on the list, your problems will evaporate, you'll find love, earn success, look better, and feel better. Being told this (or thinking this) only creates more suffering for you.

A quick sampling of trending articles include an article that lists almost *sixty* items you should buy so you can get your life in order, a list of nearly thirty mental habits that happy people practice, someone documenting the results of following a Hollywood star's diet and lifestyle regimen, and someone else reporting on his results following an action star's workout routine for a week.

Reading these or testing out new products and routines can be a lot of fun and provide a lot of inspiration. The hidden subtext is that there's a checklist for feeling better, and *you're just not good enough to get there*. We see these ways to be "better" and set unrealistic goals for ourselves. If I bought even one or two of those organizational items, I'd have more clutter that I didn't get around to using, and I wouldn't feel better organized at all. Then I would feel like I wasted money and was a failure at getting my life together. Cue depression spiral! I read articles about the habits of good friends and start to wonder if I'm letting my friends down. Meanwhile, luxury routines are almost certainly bound to feel good, but there's a reason they're accessible to celebrities—they require time and money many people don't have.

The industry may be called "self-help," but if your takeaway from the self-help industry is that you aren't good enough, you aren't practicing the right mental or physical habits, or that you need to buy more products, then that isn't self-care. There *are* positive habits you can try out or get inspired by, but the message shouldn't be that you're not trying hard enough or not doing the right things.

Try a few things, and keep what's realistic or inspiring for you. The rest might be a better fit for someone else. There's no one-size-fits-all checklist, lifestyle, routine, or product.

Where do you get strategies for self-care? What do you do for self-care?

Kaitlynn

I like to watch YouTube videos on how to stay organized, or for ways that I can reduce stress and anxiety. I like to plan out my week and keep everything I have for school organized. I also like to drink a lot of water and make sure I take some time out of my day (usually before I go to sleep) to be quiet, pray, or sometimes listen to music.

Emma

I don't usually read self-help/self-care articles online. I think many of them aren't the best option for your skin or your health. You have to find what works for you through your doctor, for example, to fit your body type or special needs.

Usually, I get my skincare and beauty advice from people at the salon. I learned what type of skin I have through them, and I learned what kind of face wash is best for me. Just because it looks good on someone else doesn't mean it's going to look good or feel right for me. I try not to look to anything online for that.

One thing I usually do for self-care is avoiding soda and artificial sweeteners. I try to limit preservatives and things like that. Even though I don't eat healthy all the time, my body feels so much better when I know I've eaten a good meal and have lots of water.

I also like making a to-do list for each day, and as the day progresses watching as that to-do list gets shorter. When I get overwhelmed, I usually listen to music and just put myself in a position where I can relax. I like my cats very much—petting them calms me down. Having a clean space makes me feel less anxious. Fuzzy blankets. Nice mugs. Chapstick. Basic but effective.

Blake

I like learning things and keeping busy with my mind, so I'll take free classes at the library.

My therapist gives me homework sometimes to do one thing each day that gives me a little good feeling no matter how small. He says even five seconds of feeling good is good enough. There are certain scents that I like, like coffee. I have a few coffeehouses that I'll go to do my homework, and I go to the ones that smell like coffee. Another scent I find relaxing is the warm smell of freshly made waffle cones. There's an ice cream place that makes fresh waffle cones and I'll go in, buy just a bottle of water or a soda so that I actually bought something, and sit there for a little bit because I feel warm when I smell waffle cones.

The last time I did that, the guy was actively making fresh waffle cones, so I asked if it was okay if I watched for a bit and if I could film him on my phone. I enjoyed it because, for a few minutes, that was all that consumed me, just following his process. He scraped the sides a lot to make sure any batter that squeezed out wasn't getting stuck there, and they cooked for a lot longer than I thought they would. It smelled amazing. Then he had this metal cone on a handle that he wrapped the waffle around while they were still hot and flexible. I watch the video sometimes and try to remember that good feeling and the good smell.

The whole process lasted maybe five minutes, but it was a time when I just got out of my head and my sad thoughts and unhappiness and watched. It also reminded me of a time when I was little, and I watched crayons being made. I got the same feeling of just watching and soaking it in without anything else being loud in my head.

CHAPTER FOURTEEN

EXPLORING MEDITATION
STRATEGIES

Meditation is a process of focusing your attention inward to your mind's processes; in the simplest terms, it is an attention exercise strengthening your ability to focus internally on your thoughts, feelings, urges, and senses. Individuals with depression might feel like they've spent an awful lot of time inside their heads. Meditation is about helping yourself to accept, notice, and be more present to what is happening in your head and body without judgment.

Our thoughts often carry us away to dark places where they keep us trapped in a spiraling loop of more similar thoughts. Meditation's goal is not to sit and focus on those thoughts, but rather to notice when your thoughts carry you away from where you want to be and gently nudge yourself back to where you were focusing before those thoughts intruded.

Just because our bodies are doing something doesn't mean our minds are in sync with it. With mindful meditation, our mind stays with what our body is doing. Meditation keeps you more aware of your bodily responses, a skill especially useful when you're in an uncomfortable situation. Practicing being present in your body with mental awareness can help you pay attention to your body's signals (that you should probably leave a situation, that something is happening that you're not comfortable with, or the opposite—that a person or place makes you feel comfortable or safe), not just in the single moment of meditation. Meditation is learning how to feel inside of your body without taking action or getting caught up in the thoughts-feelings-behaviors loop.

Mindful meditation isn't always about relaxing, just being in yourself at the moment. Doing so can often lead to relaxing, so it's doubly useful.

Doing these acceptance-based meditation exercises can build up your ability to notice what provokes your thoughts to drift or, if there's no clear trigger, to see when your thoughts have quietly tiptoed off into a dark hole. In turn, you will get better at shepherding your thoughts back like a herd of lambs that are prone to going off aimlessly. Blame, guilt, and anxiety will feed the dark spiral more. The key is nonjudgmentally guiding yourself back, not blaming yourself for having wandering thoughts or worrying about why you're drifting.

BREATHING AWARENESS

Focus your awareness on your breathing, watching the breath as it travels into your body and then out again, and repeat. Your breathing is an anchor for your thoughts, a clear pathway for them to follow that doesn't require learning any new skills. In any given moment, this is an easy path that is available for your thoughts to follow, especially since breathing is a process already happening and under way. You don't need to adjust your breathing rate or make any changes. You don't even need to close your eyes, although you can if it helps you. Just pay attention as you feel the feeling of the intake through your nose, deep down into your body, the expansion of your chest, the release back up and out, the cool flow over your lips as you exhale. Repeat this process for a few minutes. If your mind tries to drift, nudge it back to the breathing awareness.

There are multiple benefits to merely noticing your breathing. While I mentioned that you don't need to concentrate on adjusting your breath rate, counting, or holding your breath, you will almost certainly end up slowing your breathing and taking deeper breaths in a paused, thoughtful moment of focus. Doing so will lower your heart rate and blood pressure naturally, as well as replenish the oxygen in your blood expended on stress responses. The physical effect will, in turn, lower your feelings of distress. Additionally, it's incredibly difficult to hold on to distressing thoughts when your mind is preoccupied with another focus. (Again, when those thoughts do intrude, or your mind does drift elsewhere, just move it back gently without judgment.) There is also something rather soothingly hypnotic about tracing a simple, orderly path.

SENSORY AWARENESS

Much like the breathing awareness exercise, this is a way of putting your attention on something that is already taking place. In this case, pick a sense to focus on as the anchor for your thoughts. Focus only on one sense at a time, and do so nonjudgmentally.

Try to keep your details as neutral as possible. For example, if you're observing visually, you might describe a shirt by thinking about the color and what it says, but avoid thinking about how it fits or if it looks good on the person wearing it. A scent can be compared to things, but avoid judging whether it smells delicious or revolting. Try to pick as neutral an observation focus as you can.

The point of this exercise is again not explicitly relaxation, although that usually happens too. The benefit is resisting the urge to label, judge, catalog, and quantify things as good or bad. Merely paying attention to your mind in its surroundings without all the emotions that come in is a practice you will get better and better at in time.

TUNING IN

Pick a set of songs or a playlist that you like, one that listening to makes you feel good. Once a day, turn everything else off. Put your laptop away, put your cell phone down, close your door, and listen to one song—not a whole playlist, just one song—tuning into that song while tuning out everything else.

CHAPTER FIFTEEN

BUILDING YOUR
SAFETY PLAN

A safety plan is a guide to help you in moments of distress where you may be feeling urges to hurt yourself. The goal of a safety plan is to help you calm down or know who to contact so that you can return to a state of feeling safe and secure. It isn't a plan where someone else tells you what you do—it's a guide you write for yourself because you know yourself best.

Your safety plan can include a variety of things based on your needs, but try to keep it as direct as possible since it should be simple and small enough to fit on a single sheet of paper (otherwise it'll become too much trouble to flip through when you need it). Because this is a crisis plan, it isn't a long-term plan. The goal of the safety plan is to get you through the peak of your urges to self-harm until you can get more help and get to safety.

Your safety plan isn't for anyone but you, so write it down in a way that you will recognize what you mean. Information that might be useful for you to include on your safety plan includes:

- What are your red flags or warning signs that your mind is taking you to a dark place? Do you usually think about specific events, people, memories? Are there situations you gravitate toward? Do certain moods, thoughts, emotions, or habits tend to surface? List them.

- What can you do to help stay calm, safe, and stable enough to use your coping skills? Is there a place that you can go where you feel safe? Are there things to do or be around that soothe you so that

145

you don't harm yourself? Do you have any coping strategies that help you feel better in the moment? List them.

- Who can you talk to? Not necessarily someone to talk to about how you're feeling, but someone who makes you feel good. Do you have friends or family who lift your mood, distract you, or make you laugh? Are there any social settings or situations that make you feel safer and better? List them.

- What activities will distract you at the moment and prevent you from harming yourself? These should all be nonharmful activities, so taking a walk or even letting yourself scream is fine. Activities can be anything that you think will take your emotional intensity down a notch by distracting you, like playing a game or listening to music.

- Emergency numbers/mental health resources you might need. These are also useful to program into your phone.

After making a safety plan, try to keep copies of it where you'll remember to use it. It can be extremely useful to take a picture of your plan with your phone and keep it in an easily accessed favorites folder. Remember, since the plan is for you, make sure you can access it and find it quickly if ever you need it.

NOTES

CHAPTER TWO: EXPLORING DEPRESSION

1. World Health Organization, *The ICD-10 Classification of Mental and Behavioural Disorders: Clinical Descriptions and Diagnostic Guidelines.* (Geneva: World Health Organization, 1992), 119.
2. Philip S. Wang, Patricia A. Berglund, Mark Olfson, and Ronald C. Kessler, "Delays in Initial Treatment Contact after First Onset of a Mental Disorder," *Health Services Research* 39, no. 2 (2004): 398–99, https://doi.org/10.1111/j.1475-6773.2004.00234.x.

CHAPTER THREE: TAKING THE FIRST STEPS TO HEALING

1. Joseph Firth, Najma Siddiqi, Ai Koyanagi, Dan Siskind, Simon Rosenbaum, Cherrie Galletly, Stephanie Allan, et al., "The *Lancet* Psychiatry Commission: A Blueprint for Protecting Physical Health in People with Mental Illness," *Lancet Psychiatry* 6, no. 8 (2019): 675–712, https://doi.org/10.1016/S2215-0366(19)30132-4.
2. World Health Organization, "'Depression: Let's Talk' Says WHO, as Depression Tops List of Causes of Ill Health," last modified March 30, 2017, https://www.who.int/news-room/detail/30-03-2017--depression -let-s-talk-says-who-as-depression-tops-list-of-causes-of-ill-health.

CHAPTER FOUR: LOOKING AT THE NUMBERS

1. OECD, *PISA 2018 Results (Volume III): What School Life Means for Students' Lives* (Paris: OECD Publishing, 2019), https://doi.org/10.1787/acd78851-en.
2. OECD, *PISA 2018 Results.*
3. A. W. Geiger and Leslie Davis, "A Growing Number of American Teenagers—Particularly Girls—Are Facing Depression," Pew Research Center, last modified July 12, 2019, https://www.pewresearch.org/fact-tank/2019/07/12/a-growing-number-of-american-teenagers-particularly-girls-are-facing-depression/.
4. P. Patalay and E. Fitzsimons, "Mental Ill-Health among Children of the New Century: Trends across Childhood with a Focus on Age 14," Centre for Longitudinal Studies, last modified September 20, 2017, https://cls.ucl.ac.uk/wp-content/uploads/2017/11/Briefing-paper-mental-ill-health-among-children-of-the-new-century-September-20-2017.pdf.
5. Juliana Menasce Horowitz and Nikki Graf, "Most U.S. Teens See Anxiety and Depression as a Major Problem among Their Peers," Pew Research Center, last modified February 20, 2019, https://www.pewsocialtrends.org/2019/02/20/most-u-s-teens-see-anxiety-and-depression-as-a-major-problem-among-their-peers/.
6. Child Mind Institute, *2017 Children's Mental Health Report*, last modified September 2017, https://childmind.org/report/2017-childrens-mental-health-report/.
7. Melonie Heron, "Deaths: Leading Causes for 2017," National Center for Health Statistics, last modified June 24, 2019, https://www.cdc.gov/nchs/data/nvsr/nvsr68/nvsr68_06-508.pdf; Statistics Canada, "Table 13-10-0394-01: Leading Causes of Death, Total Population, by Age Group," last modified November 30, 2019, https://www150.statcan.gc.ca/t1/tbl1/en/tv.action?pid=1310039401&pickMemberspercent5B0percent5D=2.4&pickMemberspercent5B1percent5D=3.1.
8. Vasita Patel, "Deaths Registered in England and Wales (Series DR): 2017," Office for National Statistics, last modified October 23, 2018, https://www.ons.gov.uk/peoplepopulationandcommunity/birthsdeathsandmarriages/deaths/bulletins/deathsregisteredinenglandandwalesseriesdr/2017.

9. Bridget J. Goosby, Anna Bellatorre, Katrina M. Walsemann, and Jacob E. Cheadle, "Adolescent Loneliness and Health in Early Adulthood," *Sociological Inquiry* 83, no. 4 (2013): 507–8, https://doi.org/10.1111/soin.12018; Raheel Mushtaq, Sheikh Shoib, Tabindah Shah, and Sahil Mushtaq, "Relationship between Loneliness, Psychiatric Disorders and Physical Health? A Review on the Psychological Aspects of Loneliness," *Journal of Clinical and Diagnostic Research* 8, no. 9 (2014): 1. https://doi.org/10.7860/JCDR/2014/10077.4828.

10. Child Mind Institute, *2018 Children's Mental Health Report: Understanding Anxiety in Children and Teens*, last modified September 2018, https://childmind.org/our-impact/childrens-mental-health-report/2018report/.

11. Child Mind Institute, *2018 Children's Mental Health Report*.

CHAPTER FIVE: THE PROBLEM WITH STRESS

1. American Psychological Association, *Stress in America: Generation Z*, last modified October 2018, https://www.apa.org/news/press/releases/stress/2018/stress-gen-z.pdf.

2. American Psychological Association, *Stress in America: Are Teens Adopting Adults' Stress Habits?*, last modified February 2014, https://www.apa.org/news/press/releases/stress/2013/stress-report.pdf.

CHAPTER SEVEN: THE STRESSORS

1. Juliana Menasce Horowitz and Nikki Graf, "Most U.S. Teens See Anxiety and Depression as a Major Problem among Their Peers," Pew Research Center, last modified February 20, 2019, https://www.pewsocialtrends.org/2019/02/20/most-u-s-teens-see-anxiety-and-depression-as-a-major-problem-among-their-peers/.

2. American Psychological Association, "Stress in America: Generation Z," last modified October 2018, https://www.apa.org/news/press/releases/stress/2018/stress-gen-z.pdf.

CHAPTER NINE: THE PROBLEM
WITH FORCED POSITIVITY

1. Susan David, "The Gift and Power of Emotional Courage," November 2017, TED video, 13:53, https://www.ted.com/talks/susan_david_the_gift_and_power_of_emotional_courage?language=en.
2. Brett Q. Ford, Phoebe Lam, Oliver P. John, and Iris B. Mauss, "The Psychological Health Benefits of Accepting Negative Emotions and Thoughts: Laboratory, Diary, and Longitudinal Evidence," supplement, *Journal of Personality and Social Psychology* 115, no. 6 (2018): 1075–92, https://doi.org/10.1037/pspp0000157.supp.

CHAPTER ELEVEN:
EXPLORING HEALTHY RELATIONSHIPS

1. "Dating Abuse Statistics," loveisrespect, accessed December 11, 2019, https://www.loveisrespect.org/resources/dating-violence-statistics/.

A QUICK GUIDE
TO RESOURCES

SUICIDE CRISIS RESOURCES

Some of this information is printed elsewhere in the book, but for ease of access, mental health resources are listed here as well.

Remember, if you or a loved one is facing a mental health emergency, including thinking about suicide or self-harm, call one of the helplines listed below or go to the emergency room immediately.

Even if you feel hopeless to do anything or don't know what to do, others do know what to do. Just pause, breathe, and reach out right away to one of the resources listed here. There are many safe, confidential, free, immediate options available for you to talk, text, or chat with someone if you are in crisis.

- **In the United States**, call 911 for an emergency or the 24/7 National Suicide Prevention Hotline at 1-800-273-8255. There are options for Spanish speakers and the deaf/hard of hearing. If you feel more comfortable texting, the Crisis Text Line is a free 24/7 text message service for people in crisis. Text HOME to 741741.

- **In the United Kingdom**, call 999 for an emergency or the National Health Services' First Response Service for mental health at 111, Option 2. If you feel more comfortable texting, Shout is a free 24/7 text message service for people in crisis. Text SHOUT to 85258.

- **In Canada**, call 911 for an emergency or the 24/7 Kids Help phone service (anyone under the age of twenty) at 1-800-668-6868 or Crisis Services Canada (no age restriction) at 1-833-456-4566. Quebec residents can call Crisis Services at 1-866-277-3553. If you feel more comfortable texting, the Crisis Text Line is a free 24/7 text message service for people in crisis. Text CONNECT (for English) or PARLER (for French) to 686868.

- **In Australia**, call 000 for an emergency or the 24/7 Kids Helpline phone service (anyone under the age of twenty-five) at 1800 55 1800 or Lifeline (no age restriction) at 13 11 14. Both Lifeline (https://www.lifeline.org.au/) and Kids Helpline (https://www.kidshelpline.com.au/) have online chat features available at their websites.

ABUSIVE RELATIONSHIPS RESOURCES

If you are experiencing abuse, aren't sure if what you're experiencing is abuse, or have questions or concerns about your relationships, there are resources and advocates out there for you. Do you have questions or need to check in with someone? Do you need help? There are many safe, confidential, free, immediate options available for you to talk, text, or chat with someone if you are concerned, confused, or have questions or need to talk about your relationship dynamics.

- **In the United States**, call loveisrespect at 1-866-331-9474. There are options for Spanish speakers and the deaf/hard of hearing. There is also a live online chat available with advocates on their website at loveisrespect.org. If you feel more comfortable texting, text LOVEIS to 22522.

- **In the United Kingdom**, call the National Domestic Abuse Helpline at 0808 2000 247.

- **In Canada**, there is a range of options available for you, depending on your province. The Ending Violence Association of Canada has

a list available on their website at http://endingviolencecanada.org/
getting-help/.

- **In Australia**, call 1800RESPECT at 1800 737 732. There is also
an online chat service on their website at https://www.1800respect
.org.au/.

ADDITIONAL RESOURCES

LGBTQ+ TEENS

The Trevor Project (https://www.thetrevorproject.org/) provides a supportive, judgment-free community specifically for LGBTQ teens. It
offers crisis intervention and suicide prevention services for people under
age twenty-five.

MORE ABOUT MENTAL HEALTH

The National Alliance on Mental Illness (https://www.nami.org/) provides helpful insights and resources to support individuals with mental
illness. It has local chapters throughout the United States.

A SAFE SPACE TO TALK

The Ok2Talk website (https://ok2talk.org/) is a safe space for you to
post and read about what others are experiencing.

BIBLIOGRAPHY

American Psychological Association. *Stress in America: Are Teens Adopting Adults' Stress Habits?* Last modified February 2014. https://www.apa.org/news/press/releases/stress/2013/stress-report.pdf.

———. *Stress in America: Generation Z.* Last modified October 2018. https://www.apa.org/news/press/releases/stress/2018/stress-gen-z.pdf.

Child Mind Institute. *2017 Children's Mental Health Report.* Last modified September 2017. https://childmind.org/report/2017-childrens-mental-health-report/.

———. *2018 Children's Mental Health Report: Understanding Anxiety in Children and Teens.* Last modified September 2018. https://childmind.org/our-impact/childrens-mental-health-report/2018report/.

Dandona, Rakhi. "Mind and Body Go Together: The Need for Integrated Care." *Lancet Psychiatry* 6, no. 8 (2019): 638–39. https://doi.org/10.1016/S2215-0366(19)30251-2.

David, Susan. "The Gift and Power of Emotional Courage." November 2017. TED video, 13:53. https://www.ted.com/talks/susan_david_the_gift_and_power_of_emotional_courage?language=en.

Firth, Joseph, Najma Siddiqi, Ai Koyanagi, Dan Siskind, Simon Rosenbaum, Cherrie Galletly, Stephanie Allan, et al. "The *Lancet* Psychiatry Commission: A Blueprint for Protecting Physical Health in People with Mental Illness." *Lancet Psychiatry* 6, no. 8 (2019): 675–712. https://doi.org/10.1016/S2215-0366(19)30132-4.

Ford, Brett Q., Phoebe Lam, Oliver P. John, and Iris B. Mauss. "The Psychological Health Benefits of Accepting Negative Emotions and Thoughts: Laboratory, Diary, and Longitudinal Evidence."

Supplement, *Journal of Personality and Social Psychology* 115, no. 6 (2018): 1075–92. https://doi.org/10.1037/pspp0000157.supp.

Geiger, A. W., and Leslie Davis. "A Growing Number of American Teen-agers—Particularly Girls—Are Facing Depression." Pew Research Center. Last modified July 12, 2019. https://www.pewresearch.org/fact-tank/2019/07/12/a-growing-number-of-american-teenagers-particularly-girls-are-facing-depression/.

Goosby, Bridget J., Anna Bellatorre, Katrina M. Walsemann, and Jacob E. Cheadle. "Adolescent Loneliness and Health in Early Adult-hood." *Sociological Inquiry* 83, no. 4 (2013): 505–36. https://doi.org/10.1111/soin.12018.

Heron, Melonie. "Deaths: Leading Causes for 2017." National Center for Health Statistics. Last modified June 24, 2019. https://www.cdc.gov/nchs/data/nvsr/nvsr68/nvsr68_06-508.pdf.

Horowitz, Juliana Menasce, and Nikki Graf. "Most U.S. Teens See Anxiety and Depression as a Major Problem among Their Peers." Pew Research Center. Last modified February 20, 2019. https://www.pewsocialtrends.org/2019/02/20/most-u-s-teens-see-anxiety-and-depression-as-a-major-problem-among-their-peers/.

Loveisrespect. "Dating Abuse Statistics." Loveisrespect.org. Accessed December 11, 2019. https://www.loveisrespect.org/resources/dating-violence-statistics/.

Mushtaq, Raheel, Sheikh Shoib, Tabindah Shah, and Sahil Mushtaq. "Relationship between Loneliness, Psychiatric Disorders and Phys-ical Health? A Review on the Psychological Aspects of Loneliness." *Journal of Clinical and Diagnostic Research* 8, no. 9 (2014): 1–4. https://doi.org/10.7860/JCDR/2014/10077.4828.

OECD. *PISA 2018 Results (Volume III): What School Life Means for Students' Lives.* Paris, OECD Publishing, 2019. https://doi.org/10.1787/acd78851-en.

Patalay, P., and E. Fitzsimons. "Mental Ill-Health among Children of the New Century: Trends across Childhood with a Focus on Age 14." Centre for Longitudinal Studies. Last modified September 20, 2017. https://cls.ucl.ac.uk/wp-content/uploads/2017/11/Briefing

-paper-mental-ill-health-among-children-of-the-new-century-Sept
ember-20-2017.pdf.

Patalay, Praveetha, and Suzanne H. Gage. "Changes in Millennial
Adolescent Mental Health and Health Related Behaviours over
10 Years: A Population Cohort Comparison Study." *International
Journal of Epidemiology* 48, no. 5 (2019): 1650–64. https://doi
.org/10.1093/ije/dyz006.

Patel, Vasita. "Deaths Registered in England and Wales (Series DR):
2017." Office for National Statistics. Last modified October 23,
2018. https://www.ons.gov.uk/peoplepopulationandcommunity/
birthsdeathsandmarriages/deaths/bulletins/deathsregisteredinen
glandandwalesseriesdr/2017.

Statistics Canada. "Table 13-10-0394-01: Leading Causes of Death,
Total Population, by Age Group." Last modified November 30,
2019. https://www150.statcan.gc.ca/t1/tbl1/en/tv.action?pid=131
0039401&pickMembers%5B0%5D=2.4&pickMembers%
5B1%5D=3.1.

Wang, Philip S., Patricia A. Berglund, Mark Olfson, and Ronald C.
Kessler. "Delays in Initial Treatment Contact after First Onset of a
Mental Disorder." *Health Services Research* 39, no. 2 (2004): 393–
416. https://doi.org/10.1111/j.1475-6773.2004.00234.x.

World Health Organization. "'Depression: Let's Talk' Says WHO, as
Depression Tops List of Causes of Ill Health." World Health Organization. Last modified March 30, 2017. https://www.who.int/
news-room/detail/30-03-2017--depression-let-s-talk-says-who-as
-depression-tops-list-of-causes-of-ill-health.

———. *The ICD-10 Classification of Mental and Behavioural Disorders:
Clinical Descriptions and Diagnostic Guidelines.* Geneva: World
Health Organization, 1992.

INDEX

ABOUT THE AUTHOR

Christie Cognevich received her PhD in literature from Louisiana State University and is earning an MFA in writing for children and young adults from Vermont College of Fine Arts. She teaches high school English and creative writing in New Orleans, Louisiana, where she lives with her two cats named after dead poets. In addition to teaching and writing, she enjoys graphic design. She can be found online at christiecognevich.com.